AF382811

# MILIN

# COOKBOOK FOR BEGINNERS

## QUICK, EASY AND FLAVORFUL RECIPES TO AIR FRYING, BAKE, GRILL AND ROAST FOR EASY AND TASTY MEALS

**JIMMY DEHART**

**Copyright © 2021 by Jimmy Dehart- All rights reserved.**

The content contained within this book may not be reproduced, duplicated, or transmitted without direct written permission from the author or the publisher. Under no circumstances will any blame or legal responsibility be held against the publisher, or author, for any damages, reparation, or monetary loss due to the information contained within this book, either directly or indirectly.

**Legal Notice**: This book is copyright protected. It is only for personal use. You cannot amend, distribute, sell, use, quote or paraphrase any part, or the content within this book, without the consent of the author or publisher.

**Disclaimer Notice**: Please note the information contained within this document is for educational and entertainment purposes only. All effort has been executed to present accurate, up to date, reliable, complete information. No warranties of any kind are declared or implied. Readers acknowledge that the author is not engaged in the rendering of legal, financial, medical, or professional advice. The content within this book has been derived from various sources. Please consult a licensed professional before attempting any techniques outlined in this book. By reading this document, the reader agrees that under no circumstances is the author responsible for any losses, direct or indirect, that are incurred as a result of the use of the information contained within this document, including, but not limited to, errors, omissions, or inaccuracies.

# CONTENTS

# INTRODUCTION

## The Operation Principle of MILIN Air Fryer

What's the secret to this appliance's magic? When you break it down, an air fryer is essentially a miniature convection oven that evenly circulates hot air around your food. Air fryers contain a fan that rapidly moves the heated air around, helping your food to crisp up without much additional oil. It also has the ability to reach very high temperatures (with some models getting up to 430F°) enhancing its ability to quickly cook foods. The device is ideal for anyone keeping a close eye on their fat consumption, as you only need a thin coat of oil on the food or on the cookware surface to prevent sticking and achieve a golden, crispy crunch. Not only does it fry, but the air fryer can also mimic other cooking functions such as baking, grilling and roasting.

Keep in mind that an air fryer is ideal for making foods in small quantities simply because the appliance does not have the physical capacity to hold a lot of food at one time. Most models can hold a from 3.5 quarts to 5.5 quarts in their fry baskets. The fry basket is the main accessory that comes with an air fryer, but some models can include other elements such as a baking pan or roasting rack. Being that the air fryer is similar to a convection oven (but way smaller), it can save you time (and electricity) over heating up your standard oven. It cooks food freakishly fast and the clean up fuss-free.

# The Advantages of MILIN Air Fryer

Air fryers have gained popularity in recent months due to the increased health awareness and more people taking deliberate action to ensure they live a healthy lifestyle. These air fryers have a lot of benefits to offer, some of which are highlighted below:

## 1. Cook Multiple Dishes

You can cook multiple dishes at once with an air fryer which would save you a lot of time. This is like having a skillet, a deep fryer, a toaster, and an oven together in one machine. There are also several healthy dishes you can make with it; for example, the air fryer salmon recipes. Salmon is known for its many health benefits and with an air fryer in place, you can worry less about ever having trouble cooking this fish. Other recipes you can try include the Crispy Air Fryer Baked Potatoes, Crispy Air Fryer Bacon, Air Fryer Mozzarella Sticks, Air Fryer Chocolate Chip Cookies, and Air Fryer Buttermilk Fried Chicken, among others.

## 2. It Helps Promote Weight Loss

Several studies have shown how fried foods can increase the risk of weight gain and obesity and other cardiovascular problems. In a study conducted in 2019 on mortality in women in the United States, it was found that "the frequent consumption of fried foods, especially fried chicken and fried fish/shellfish, was associated with a higher risk of all cause and cardiovascular mortality in women in the US".

However, you don't have to completely give up your favorite meals that require deep frying. A healthier option will be to use an air fryer for all fried meals, as it reduces your regular take of unhealthy oils, which promotes weight loss. Weight loss also reduces your risk of other health complications, including cardiovascular disease.

## 3. It is Safe to Use

One of the major troubles of deep frying is the risk of hot oil accidents or the consistent splashing of oil while frying. With air fryers, you can worry less about this, as there's no risk of spilling or splashing of oil. You also do not have to worry about your kids being around the kitchen. It has an auto shut feature that is activated once cooking is completed, so you don't have to worry about overheating or burnt food.

The safety standards of air fryers make them more suitable compared to the traditional deep frying method.

## 4. It Reduces the Risk of Toxic Acrylamide Formation

Acrylamide formation is mostly caused by high-temperature cooking such as frying, roasting, or baking. This compound is dangerous and increases the risk of various cancers, including endometrial, ovarian, pancreatic, breast, and esophageal cancers. You can however reduce this risk by using an air fryer.

# The Preparations for Air-Frying Use

## 1. Prepare the Food You'll Be Cooking

Like in any other cooking methodology, the very first thing you should do is to prepare the food you'll be cooking. Most ingredients aren't always bite size and ready to cook, so you have to do the washing, peeling, and chopping in this step, mostly. If you're going to cook a ready-to-eat frozen product, all you'll really need to do is take it out of the freezer. Most air fryers will be able to cook it nicely straight out of the fridge, making them very convenient options for quick meals.

Those who like to make their fried dishes with batter, check with your air fryer's manufacturer whether they can work with such before doing anything. If you're going to use wet ingredients like meat and freshly washed veggies, make sure to pat them dry first as well. This way, your air fryer won't have to work extra to dry the food and get to use its capacity to actually cook your food efficiently.

You can also wrap your ingredients with aluminum foil if you want to make the most out of your cooking basket's space. This will let you cook two different dishes in one go without the need for any accessory.

## 2. Prepare Your MILIN Air Fryer

Once your ingredients are prepped, the next step is to prepare your air fryer. If you're going to use accessories, grab them now. It's best to have them on hand so you can also clean them up if they need some rinsing.

You should also check if the air fryer is clean and dry before plugging it in and starting it up. Crusted old food can affect the taste and smell of your dish, so it's best to make sure that your air fryer is completely clean before using it.

## 3. Preheat Your MILIN Air Fryer

While this is still a part of preparing your appliance for cooking, it's still worth a special mention because it's something a lot of people tend to forget.

To preheat, set the appliance to the highest heat level and leave it on for five minutes. That will do the trick to heat up your unit nicely in just a short amount of time.

## 4. Load the Ingredients into the MILIN Air Fryer

Once the air fryer is already hot, it's ready to start cooking. Load the ingredients into its cooking basket. Make sure to use the right accessories if you intend to use them. Also, make sure to use them properly so you can make the most out of them.

## 5. Make Sure Not to Crowd the Cooking Basket

While loading your ingredients into the air fryer, another key trick how to use an air fryer is to avoid crowding the basket. Your ingredients will need all the space it can get so it can be exposed to hot air, while the hot air also needs room to move around.

Don't think that you'll get away with filling the basket to the brim as that will only lead to an undercooked mess.

## 6. Add a Bit of Oil to the Cooking Basket

The next thing you should do is to add some oil into your air fryer. While you can skip the oil entirely, it's still useful if you want to make sure that your ingredients won't stick together or to the basket while cooking. It will also give your dish the fried taste that only cooking with oil can give.

# The Tips for Cleaning MILIN Air Fryer

After your delicious meal is finished, it's time to clean your air fryer. We recommend cleaning your air fryer every time you use it, but the process of cleaning is not as daunting as you think.

➢ Unplug air fryer and take out the basket and the pan.

➢ Take a microfiber cloth and dampen it with hot water to clean the exterior of the appliance. Then, to clean the interior take a non-abrasive sponge and scrub the interior of the fryer.

➢ Next, clean the heating element by turning your air fryer upside-down and gently scrub it with a sponge.

➢ Most of the baskets and pans are dishwasher-safe, so load them into your dishwasher and let the dishwasher do the work. If you want to clean it yourself—hot water, dish soap, and a non-abrasive sponge will do the trick.

➢ If there's tough residue on your baskets and pans, soak them in hot water for about 10 minutes. Then scrub the residue away with a non-abrasive sponge.

➢ All that's left to do is to dry your appliance. We recommend to air dry the individual parts, but you can also take a cloth to dry the appliance. After it's all dry, put it back together and you'll be ready to tackle your next tasty air fryer recipe.

# APPETIZERS AND SNACKS

## "fried" Pickles With Homemade Ranch

Servings: 8

Cooking Time: 8 Minutes

**Ingredients:**

- ➢ 1 cup all-purpose flour
- ➢ 2 teaspoons dried dill
- ➢ ½ teaspoon paprika
- ➢ ¾ cup buttermilk
- ➢ 1 egg
- ➢ 4 large kosher dill pickles, sliced ¼-inch thick
- ➢ 2 cups panko breadcrumbs

**Directions:**

1. Preheat the air fryer to 380°F.
2. In a medium bowl, whisk together the flour, dill, paprika, buttermilk, and egg.
3. Dip and coat thick slices of dill pickles into the batter. Next, dredge into the panko breadcrumbs.
4. Place a single layer of breaded pickles into the air fryer basket. Spray the pickles with cooking spray. Cook for 4 minutes, turn over, and cook another 4 minutes. Repeat until all the pickle chips have been cooked.

# Loaded Potato Skins

Servings: 8

Cooking Time: 8 Minutes

**Ingredients:**

- 12 round baby potatoes
- 3 ounces cream cheese
- 4 slices cooked bacon, crumbled or chopped
- 2 green onions, finely chopped
- ½ cup grated cheddar cheese, divided
- ¼ cup sour cream
- 1 tablespoon milk
- 2 teaspoons hot sauce

**Directions:**

1. Preheat the air fryer to 320°F.

2. Poke holes into the baby potatoes with a fork. Place the potatoes onto a microwave-safe plate and microwave on high for 4 to 5 minutes, or until soft to squeeze. Let the potatoes cool until they're safe to handle, about 5 minutes.

3. Meanwhile, in a medium bowl, mix together the cream cheese, bacon, green onions, and ¼ cup of the cheddar cheese; set aside.

4. Slice the baby potatoes in half. Using a spoon, scoop out the pulp, leaving enough pulp on the inside to retain the shape of the potato half. Place the potato pulp into the cream cheese mixture and mash together with a fork. Using a spoon, refill the potato halves with filling.

5. Place the potato halves into the air fryer basket and top with the remaining ¼ cup of cheddar cheese.

6. Cook the loaded baked potato bites in batches for 8 minutes.

7. Meanwhile, make the sour cream sauce. In a small bowl, whisk together the sour cream, milk, and hot sauce. Add more hot sauce if desired.

8. When the potatoes have all finished cooking, place them onto a serving platter and serve with sour cream sauce drizzled over the top or as a dip.

# Cinnamon Pita Chips

Servings: 4

Cooking Time: 6 Minutes

**Ingredients:**

- ➢ 2 tablespoons sugar
- ➢ 2 teaspoons cinnamon
- ➢ 2 whole 6-inch pitas, whole grain or white
- ➢ oil for misting or cooking spray

**Directions:**

1.  Mix sugar and cinnamon together.
2.  Cut each pita in half and each half into 4 wedges. Break apart each wedge at the fold.
3.  Mist one side of pita wedges with oil or cooking spray. Sprinkle them all with half of the cinnamon sugar.
4.  Turn the wedges over, mist the other side with oil or cooking spray, and sprinkle with the remaining cinnamon sugar.
5.  Place pita wedges in air fryer basket and cook at 330°F for 2minutes.
6.  Shake basket and cook 2 more minutes. Shake again, and if needed cook 2 more minutes, until crisp. Watch carefully because at this point they will cook very quickly.

# Homemade French Fries

Servings: 2

Cooking Time: 25 Minutes

**Ingredients:**

- 2 to 3 russet potatoes, peeled and cut into ½-inch sticks
- 2 to 3 teaspoons olive or vegetable oil
- salt

**Directions:**

1. Bring a large saucepan of salted water to a boil on the stovetop while you peel and cut the potatoes. Blanch the potatoes in the boiling salted water for 4 minutes while you Preheat the air fryer to 400°F. Strain the potatoes and rinse them with cold water. Dry them well with a clean kitchen towel.

2. Toss the dried potato sticks gently with the oil and place them in the air fryer basket. Air-fry for 25 minutes, shaking the basket a few times while the fries cook to help them brown evenly. Season the fries with salt mid-way through cooking and serve them warm with tomato ketchup, Sriracha mayonnaise or a mix of lemon zest, Parmesan cheese and parsley.

# Fried Bananas

Servings: 4

Cooking Time: 8 Minutes

**Ingredients:**

- ½ cup panko breadcrumbs
- ½ cup sweetened coconut flakes
- ¼ cup sliced almonds
- ½ cup cornstarch
- 2 egg whites
- 1 tablespoon water
- 2 firm bananas
- oil for misting or cooking spray

**Directions:**

1. In food processor, combine panko, coconut, and almonds. Process to make small crumbs.

2. Place cornstarch in a shallow dish. In another shallow dish, beat together the egg whites and water until slightly foamy.

3. Preheat air fryer to 390°F.

4. Cut bananas in half crosswise. Cut each half in quarters lengthwise so you have 16 "sticks."

5. Dip banana sticks in cornstarch and tap to shake off excess. Then dip bananas in egg wash and roll in crumb mixture. Spray with oil.

6. Place bananas in air fryer basket in single layer and cook for 4minutes. If any spots have not browned, spritz with oil. Cook for 4 more minutes, until golden brown and crispy.

7. Repeat step 6 to cook remaining bananas.

# Eggplant Fries

Servings: 4

Cooking Time: 8 Minutes

**Ingredients:**

- 1 medium eggplant
- 1 teaspoon ground coriander
- 1 teaspoon cumin
- 1 teaspoon garlic powder
- ½ teaspoon salt
- 1 cup crushed panko breadcrumbs
- 1 large egg
- 2 tablespoons water
- oil for misting or cooking spray

**Directions:**

1. Peel and cut the eggplant into fat fries, ⅜- to ½-inch thick.
2. Preheat air fryer to 390°F.
3. In a small cup, mix together the coriander, cumin, garlic, and salt.
4. Combine 1 teaspoon of the seasoning mix and panko crumbs in a shallow dish.
5. Place eggplant fries in a large bowl, sprinkle with remaining seasoning, and stir well to combine.
6. Beat eggs and water together and pour over eggplant fries. Stir to coat.
7. Remove eggplant from egg wash, shaking off excess, and roll in panko crumbs.
8. Spray with oil.
9. Place half of the fries in air fryer basket. You should have only a single layer, but it's fine if they overlap a little.
10. Cook for 5minutes. Shake basket, mist lightly with oil, and cook 3 minutes longer, until browned and crispy.
11. Repeat step 10 to cook remaining eggplant.

# Corn Dog Muffins

Servings: 8

Cooking Time: 10 Minutes

**Ingredients:**

- 1¼ cups sliced kosher hotdogs (3 or 4, depending on size)
- ½ cup flour
- ½ cup yellow cornmeal
- 2 teaspoons baking powder
- ½ cup skim milk
- 1 egg
- 2 tablespoons canola oil
- 8 foil muffin cups, paper liners removed
- cooking spray
- mustard or your favorite dipping sauce

**Directions:**

1. Slice each hot dog in half lengthwise, then cut in ¼-inch half-moon slices. Set aside.
2. Preheat air fryer to 390°F.
3. In a large bowl, stir together flour, cornmeal, and baking powder.
4. In a small bowl, beat together the milk, egg, and oil until just blended.
5. Pour egg mixture into dry ingredients and stir with a spoon to mix well.
6. Stir in sliced hot dogs.
7. Spray the foil cups lightly with cooking spray.
8. Divide mixture evenly into muffin cups.
9. Place 4 muffin cups in the air fryer basket and cook for 5 minutes.
10. Reduce temperature to 360°F and cook 5 minutes or until toothpick inserted in center of muffin comes out clean.
11. Repeat steps 9 and 10 to bake remaining corn dog muffins.
12. Serve with mustard or other sauces for dipping.

# Muffuletta Sliders

Servings: 8

Cooking Time: 7 Minutes

**Ingredients:**

- ¼ pound thin-sliced deli ham
- ¼ pound thin-sliced pastrami
- 4 ounces low-fat mozzarella cheese, grated or sliced thin
- 8 slider buns
- olive oil for misting
- 1 tablespoon sesame seeds
- Olive Mix
- ¼ cup sliced black olives
- ½ cup sliced green olives with pimentos
- ¼ cup chopped kalamata olives
- 1 teaspoon red wine vinegar
- ¼ teaspoon basil
- ⅛ teaspoon garlic powder

**Directions:**

1. In a small bowl, stir together all the Olive Mix ingredients.
2. Divide the meats and cheese into 8 equal portions. To assemble sliders, stack in this order: bottom bun, ham, pastrami, 2 tablespoons olive mix, cheese, top bun.
3. Mist tops of sliders lightly with oil. Sprinkle with sesame seeds.
4. Cooking 4 at a time, place sliders in air fryer basket and cook at 360°F for 7 minutes to melt cheese and heat through.

# Sweet And Salty Snack Mix

Servings: 10

Cooking Time: 12 Minutes

**Ingredients:**

➢ ½ cup honey

➢ 3 tablespoons butter, melted

➢ 1 teaspoon salt

➢ 2 cups sesame sticks

➢ 1 cup pepitas (pumpkin seeds)

➢ 2 cups granola

➢ 1 cup cashews

➢ 2 cups crispy corn puff cereal (Kix® or Corn Pops®)

➢ 2 cups mini pretzel crisps

➢ 1 cup dried cherries

**Directions:**

1.  Combine the honey, butter and salt in a small bowl or measuring cup and stir until combined.

2.  Combine the sesame sticks, pepitas, granola, cashews, corn puff cereal and pretzel crisps in a large bowl. Pour the honey mixture over the top and toss to combine.

3.  Preheat air fryer to 370°F.

4.  Air-fry the snack mix in two batches. Place half the mixture in the air fryer basket and air-fry for 12 minutes, or until the snack mix is lightly toasted. Toss the basket several times throughout the process so that the mix cooks evenly and doesn't get too dark on top.

5.  Transfer the snack mix to a cookie sheet and let it cool completely. Mix in the dried cherries and store the mix in an airtight container for up to a week or two.

# Rumaki

Servings: 24

Cooking Time: 12 Minutes

**Ingredients:**

- ➢ 10 ounces raw chicken livers
- ➢ 1 can sliced water chestnuts, drained
- ➢ ¼ cup low-sodium teriyaki sauce
- ➢ 12 slices turkey bacon
- ➢ toothpicks

**Directions:**

1. Cut livers into 1½-inch pieces, trimming out tough veins as you slice.
2. Place livers, water chestnuts, and teriyaki sauce in small container with lid. If needed, add another tablespoon of teriyaki sauce to make sure livers are covered. Refrigerate for 1 hour.
3. When ready to cook, cut bacon slices in half crosswise.
4. Wrap 1 piece of liver and 1 slice of water chestnut in each bacon strip. Secure with toothpick.
5. When you have wrapped half of the livers, place them in the air fryer basket in a single layer.
6. Cook at 390°F for 12 minutes, until liver is done and bacon is crispy.
7. While first batch cooks, wrap the remaining livers. Repeat step 6 to cook your second batch.

# **Crispy Wontons**

Servings: 8                                      Cooking Time: 10 Minutes

**Ingredients:**

- ½ cup refried beans
- 3 tablespoons salsa
- ¼ cup canned artichoke hearts, drained and patted dry
- ¼ cup frozen spinach, defrosted and squeezed dry
- 2 ounces cream cheese
- 1½ teaspoons dried oregano, divided
- ¼ teaspoon garlic powder
- ¼ teaspoon onion powder
- ½ teaspoon salt
- ¼ cup chopped pepperoni
- ¼ cup grated mozzarella cheese
- 1 tablespoon grated Parmesan
- 2 ounces cream cheese
- ½ teaspoon dried oregano
- 32 wontons
- 1 cup water

**Directions:**

1. Preheat the air fryer to 370°F.

2. In a medium bowl, mix together the refried beans and salsa.

3. In a second medium bowl, mix together the artichoke hearts, spinach, cream cheese, oregano, garlic powder, onion powder, and salt.

4. In a third medium bowl, mix together the pepperoni, mozzarella cheese, Parmesan cheese, cream cheese, and the remaining ½ teaspoon of oregano.

5. Get a towel lightly damp with water and ring it out. While working with the wontons, leave the unfilled wontons under the damp towel so they don't dry out.

6. Working with 8 wontons at a time, place 2 teaspoons of one of the fillings into the center of the wonton, rotating among the different fillings (one filling per wonton). Working one at a time, use a pastry brush, dip the pastry brush into the water, and brush the edges of the dough with the water. Fold the dough in half to form a triangle and set aside. Continue until 8 wontons are formed. Spray the wontons with cooking spray and cover with a dry towel. Repeat until all 32 wontons have been filled.

7. Place the wontons into the air fryer basket, leaving space between the wontons, and cook for 5 minutes. Turn over and check for brownness, and then cook for another 5 minutes.

# POULTRY RECIPES

## Fiesta Chicken Plate

Servings: 4

Cooking Time: 15 Minutes

**Ingredients:**

- 1 pound boneless, skinless chicken breasts (2 large breasts)
- 2 tablespoons lime juice
- 1 teaspoon cumin
- ½ teaspoon salt
- ½ cup grated Pepper Jack cheese
- 1 16-ounce can refried beans
- ½ cup salsa
- 2 cups shredded lettuce
- 1 medium tomato, chopped
- 2 avocados, peeled and sliced
- 1 small onion, sliced into thin rings
- sour cream
- tortilla chips (optional)

**Directions:**

1. Split each chicken breast in half lengthwise.
2. Mix lime juice, cumin, and salt together and brush on all surfaces of chicken breasts.
3. Place in air fryer basket and cook at 390°F for 15 minutes, until well done.
4. Divide the cheese evenly over chicken breasts and cook for an additional minute to melt cheese.
5. While chicken is cooking, heat refried beans on stovetop or in microwave.
6. When ready to serve, divide beans among 4 plates. Place chicken breasts on top of beans and spoon salsa over. Arrange the lettuce, tomatoes, and avocados artfully on each plate and scatter with the onion rings.
7. Pass sour cream at the table and serve with tortilla chips if desired.

# Chicken Flautas

Servings: 6

Cooking Time: 8 Minutes

**Ingredients:**

- ➢ 6 tablespoons whipped cream cheese
- ➢ 1 cup shredded cooked chicken
- ➢ 6 tablespoons mild pico de gallo salsa
- ➢ ⅓ cup shredded Mexican cheese
- ➢ ½ teaspoon taco seasoning
- ➢ Six 8-inch flour tortillas
- ➢ 2 cups shredded lettuce
- ➢ ½ cup guacamole

**Directions:**

1. Preheat the air fryer to 370°F.

2. In a large bowl, mix the cream cheese, chicken, salsa, shredded cheese, and taco seasoning until well combined.

3. Lay the tortillas on a flat surface. Divide the cheese-and-chicken mixture into 6 equal portions; then place the mixture in the center of the tortillas, spreading evenly, leaving about 1 inch from the edge of the tortilla.

4. Spray the air fryer basket with olive oil spray. Roll up the flautas and place them edge side down into the basket. Lightly mist the top of the flautas with olive oil spray.

5. Repeat until the air fryer basket is full. You may need to cook these in batches, depending on the size of your air fryer.

6. Cook for 7 minutes, or until the outer edges are browned.

7. Remove from the air fryer basket and serve warm over a bed of shredded lettuce with guacamole on top.

# Spinach And Feta Stuffed Chicken Breasts

Servings: 4

Cooking Time: 27 Minutes

**Ingredients:**

- ➤ 1 (10-ounce) package frozen spinach, thawed and drained well
- ➤ 1 cup feta cheese, crumbled
- ➤ ½ teaspoon freshly ground black pepper
- ➤ 4 boneless chicken breasts
- ➤ salt and freshly ground black pepper
- ➤ 1 tablespoon olive oil

**Directions:**

1. Prepare the filling. Squeeze out as much liquid as possible from the thawed spinach. Rough chop the spinach and transfer it to a mixing bowl with the feta cheese and the freshly ground black pepper.

2. Prepare the chicken breast. Place the chicken breast on a cutting board and press down on the chicken breast with one hand to keep it stabilized. Make an incision about 1-inch long in the fattest side of the breast. Move the knife up and down inside the chicken breast, without poking through either the top or the bottom, or the other side of the breast. The inside pocket should be about 3-inches long, but the opening should only be about 1-inch wide. If this is too difficult, you can make the incision longer, but you will have to be more careful when cooking the chicken breast since this will expose more of the stuffing.

3. Once you have prepared the chicken breasts, use your fingers to stuff the filling into each pocket, spreading the mixture down as far as you can.

4. Preheat the air fryer to 380°F.

5. Lightly brush or spray the air fryer basket and the chicken breasts with olive oil. Transfer two of the stuffed chicken breasts to the air fryer. Air-fry for 12 minutes, turning the chicken breasts over halfway through the cooking time. Remove the chicken to a resting plate and air-fry the second two breasts for 12 minutes. Return the first batch of chicken to the air fryer with the second batch and air-fry for 3 more minutes. When the chicken is cooked, an instant read thermometer should register 165°F in the thickest part of the chicken, as well as in the stuffing.

6. Remove the chicken breasts and let them rest on a cutting board for 2 to 3 minutes. Slice the chicken on the bias and serve with the slices fanned out.

# Chicken Adobo

Servings: 6

Cooking Time: 12 Minutes

**Ingredients:**

- ➢  6 boneless chicken thighs
- ➢  ¼ cup soy sauce or tamari
- ➢  ½ cup rice wine vinegar
- ➢  4 cloves garlic, minced
- ➢  ⅛ teaspoon crushed red pepper flakes
- ➢  ½ teaspoon black pepper

**Directions:**

1.  Place the chicken thighs into a resealable plastic bag with the soy sauce or tamari, the rice wine vinegar, the garlic, and the crushed red pepper flakes. Seal the bag and let the chicken marinate at least 1 hour in the refrigerator.

2.  Preheat the air fryer to 400°F.

3.  Drain the chicken and pat dry with a paper towel. Season the chicken with black pepper and liberally spray with cooking spray.

4.  Place the chicken in the air fryer basket and cook for 9 minutes, turn over at 9 minutes and check for an internal temperature of 165°F, and cook another 3 minutes.

# Chicken Nuggets

Servings: 20

Cooking Time: 14 Minutes Per Batch

**Ingredients:**

- 1 pound boneless, skinless chicken thighs, cut into 1-inch chunks
- ¾ teaspoon salt
- ½ teaspoon black pepper
- ½ teaspoon garlic powder
- ½ teaspoon onion powder
- ½ cup flour
- 2 eggs, beaten
- ½ cup panko breadcrumbs
- 3 tablespoons plain breadcrumbs
- oil for misting or cooking spray

**Directions:**

1. In the bowl of a food processor, combine chicken, ½ teaspoon salt, pepper, garlic powder, and onion powder. Process in short pulses until chicken is very finely chopped and well blended.

2. Place flour in one shallow dish and beaten eggs in another. In a third dish or plastic bag, mix together the panko crumbs, plain breadcrumbs, and ¼ teaspoon salt.

3. Shape chicken mixture into small nuggets. Dip nuggets in flour, then eggs, then panko crumb mixture.

4. Spray nuggets on both sides with oil or cooking spray and place in air fryer basket in a single layer, close but not overlapping.

5. Cook at 360°F for 10minutes. Spray with oil and cook 4 minutes, until chicken is done and coating is golden brown.

6. Repeat step 5 to cook remaining nuggets.

# Parmesan Chicken Fingers

Servings: 2

Cooking Time: 19 Minutes

**Ingredients:**

- ½ cup flour
- 1 teaspoon salt
- freshly ground black pepper
- 2 eggs, beaten
- ¾ cup seasoned panko breadcrumbs
- ¾ cup grated Parmesan cheese
- 8 chicken tenders (about 1 pound)
- OR
- 2 to 3 boneless, skinless chicken breasts, cut into strips
- vegetable oil
- marinara sauce

**Directions:**

1. Set up a dredging station. Combine the flour, salt and pepper in a shallow dish. Place the beaten eggs in second shallow dish, and combine the panko breadcrumbs and Parmesan cheese in a third shallow dish.

2. Dredge the chicken tenders in the flour mixture. Then dip them into the egg, and finally place the chicken in the breadcrumb mixture. Press the coating onto both sides of the chicken tenders. Place the coated chicken tenders on a baking sheet until they are all coated. Spray both sides of the chicken fingers with vegetable oil.

3. Preheat the air fryer to 360°F.

4. Air-fry the chicken fingers in two batches. Transfer half the chicken fingers to the air fryer basket and air-fry for 9 minutes, turning the chicken over halfway through the cooking time. When the second batch of chicken fingers has finished cooking, return the first batch to the air fryer with the second batch and air-fry for one minute to heat everything through.

5. Serve immediately with marinara sauce, honey-mustard, ketchup or your favorite dipping sauce.

# Chicken Chunks

Servings: 4

Cooking Time: 10 Minutes

**Ingredients:**

- 1 pound chicken tenders cut in large chunks, about 1½ inches
- salt and pepper
- ½ cup cornstarch
- 2 eggs, beaten
- 1 cup panko breadcrumbs
- oil for misting or cooking spray

**Directions:**

1. Season chicken chunks to your liking with salt and pepper.
2. Dip chicken chunks in cornstarch. Then dip in egg and shake off excess. Then roll in panko crumbs to coat well.
3. Spray all sides of chicken chunks with oil or cooking spray.
4. Place chicken in air fryer basket in single layer and cook at 390°F for 5minutes. Spray with oil, turn chunks over, and spray other side.
5. Cook for an additional 5minutes or until chicken juices run clear and outside is golden brown.
6. Repeat steps 4 and 5 to cook remaining chicken.

# Chicken Parmesan

Servings: 4

Cooking Time: 11 Minutes

**Ingredients:**

- 4 chicken tenders
- Italian seasoning
- salt
- ¼ cup cornstarch
- ½ cup Italian salad dressing
- ¼ cup panko breadcrumbs
- ¼ cup grated Parmesan cheese, plus more for serving
- oil for misting or cooking spray
- 8 ounces spaghetti, cooked
- 1 24-ounce jar marinara sauce

**Directions:**

1. Pound chicken tenders with meat mallet or rolling pin until about ¼-inch thick.

2. Sprinkle both sides with Italian seasoning and salt to taste.

3. Place cornstarch and salad dressing in 2 separate shallow dishes.

4. In a third shallow dish, mix together the panko crumbs and Parmesan cheese.

5. Dip flattened chicken in cornstarch, then salad dressing. Dip in the panko mixture, pressing into the chicken so the coating sticks well.

6. Spray both sides with oil or cooking spray. Place in air fryer basket in single layer.

7. Cook at 390°F for 5minutes. Spray with oil again, turning chicken to coat both sides. See tip about turning.

8. Cook for an additional 6 minutes or until chicken juices run clear and outside is browned.

9. While chicken is cooking, heat marinara sauce and stir into cooked spaghetti.

10. To serve, divide spaghetti with sauce among 4 dinner plates, and top each with a fried chicken tender. Pass additional Parmesan at the table for those who want extra cheese.

# Chicken Tikka

Servings: 4

Cooking Time: 15 Minutes

**Ingredients:**

- ¼ cup plain Greek yogurt
- 1 clove garlic, minced
- 1 tablespoon ketchup
- 1 tablespoon extra-virgin olive oil
- 1 tablespoon lemon juice
- ½ teaspoon salt
- ½ teaspoon ground cumin
- ½ teaspoon paprika
- ¼ teaspoon ground cinnamon
- ½ teaspoon ground black pepper
- ½ teaspoon cayenne pepper
- 1 pound boneless, skinless chicken thighs

**Directions:**

1.  In a large bowl, stir together the yogurt, garlic, ketchup, olive oil, lemon juice, salt, cumin, paprika, cinnamon, black pepper, and cayenne pepper until combined.

2.  Add the chicken thighs to the bow and fold the yogurt-spice mixture over the chicken thighs until they're covered with the marinade. Cover with plastic wrap and place in the refrigerator for 30 minutes.

3.  When ready to cook the chicken, remove from the refrigerator and preheat the air fryer to 370°F.

4.  Liberally spray the air fryer basket with olive oil mist. Place the chicken thighs into the air fryer basket, leaving space between the thighs to turn.

5.  Cook for 10 minutes, turn the chicken thighs, and cook another 5 minutes (or until the internal temperature reaches 165°F).

6.  Remove the chicken from the air fryer and serve warm with desired sides.

# Tandoori Chicken Legs

Servings: 2

Cooking Time: 30 Minutes

**Ingredients:**

- 1 cup plain yogurt
- 2 cloves garlic, minced
- 1 tablespoon grated fresh ginger
- 2 teaspoons paprika
- 2 teaspoons ground coriander
- 1 teaspoon ground turmeric
- 1 teaspoon salt
- ¼ teaspoon ground cayenne pepper
- juice of 1 lime
- 2 bone-in, skin-on chicken legs
- fresh cilantro leaves

**Directions:**

1. Make the marinade by combining the yogurt, garlic, ginger, spices and lime juice. Make slashes into the chicken legs to help the marinade penetrate the meat. Pour the marinade over the chicken legs, cover and let the chicken marinate for at least an hour or overnight in the refrigerator.

2. Preheat the air fryer to 380°F.

3. Transfer the chicken legs from the marinade to the air fryer basket, reserving any extra marinade. Air-fry for 15 minutes. Flip the chicken over and pour the remaining marinade over the top. Air-fry for another 15 minutes, watching to make sure it doesn't brown too much. If it does start to get too brown, you can loosely tent the chicken with aluminum foil, tucking the ends of the foil under the chicken to stop it from blowing around.

4. Serve over rice with some fresh cilantro on top.

# Jerk Turkey Meatballs

Servings: 7

Cooking Time: 8 Minutes

**Ingredients:**

- ➢ 1 pound lean ground turkey
- ➢ ¼ cup chopped onion
- ➢ 1 teaspoon minced garlic
- ➢ ½ teaspoon dried thyme
- ➢ ¼ teaspoon ground cinnamon
- ➢ 1 teaspoon cayenne pepper
- ➢ ½ teaspoon paprika
- ➢ ½ teaspoon salt
- ➢ ⅛ teaspoon black pepper
- ➢ ¼ teaspoon red pepper flakes
- ➢ 2 teaspoons brown sugar
- ➢ 1 large egg, whisked
- ➢ ⅓ cup panko breadcrumbs
- ➢ 2⅓ cups cooked brown Jasmine rice
- ➢ 2 green onions, chopped
- ➢ ¾ cup sweet onion dressing

**Directions:**

1. Preheat the air fryer to 350°F.

2. In a medium bowl, mix the ground turkey with the onion, garlic, thyme, cinnamon, cayenne pepper, paprika, salt, pepper, red pepper flakes, and brown sugar. Add the whisked egg and stir in the breadcrumbs until the turkey starts to hold together.

3. Using a 1-ounce scoop, portion the turkey into meatballs. You should get about 28 meatballs.

4. Spray the air fryer basket with olive oil spray.

5. Place the meatballs into the air fryer basket and cook for 5 minutes, shake the basket, and cook another 2 to 4 minutes (or until the internal temperature of the meatballs reaches 165°F).

6. Remove the meatballs from the basket and repeat for the remaining meatballs.

7. Serve warm over a bed of rice with chopped green onions and spicy Caribbean jerk dressing.

# Chicken Rochambeau

Servings: 4 | Cooking Time: 20 Minutes

**Ingredients:**

- 1 tablespoon butter
- 4 chicken tenders, cut in half crosswise
- salt and pepper
- ¼ cup flour
- oil for misting
- 4 slices ham, ¼- to ⅜-inches thick and large enough to cover an English muffin
- 2 English muffins, split
- Sauce
- 2 tablespoons butter
- ½ cup chopped green onions
- ½ cup chopped mushrooms
- 2 tablespoons flour
- 1 cup chicken broth
- ¼ teaspoon garlic powder
- 1½ teaspoons Worcestershire sauce

**Directions:**

1. Place 1 tablespoon of butter in air fryer baking pan and cook at 390°F for 2minutes to melt.
2. Sprinkle chicken tenders with salt and pepper to taste, then roll in the ¼ cup of flour.
3. Place chicken in baking pan, turning pieces to coat with melted butter.
4. Cook at 390°F for 5minutes. Turn chicken pieces over, and spray tops lightly with olive oil. Cook 5minutes longer or until juices run clear. The chicken will not brown.
5. While chicken is cooking, make the sauce: In a medium saucepan, melt the 2 tablespoons of butter.
6. Add onions and mushrooms and sauté until tender, about 3minutes.
7. Stir in the flour. Gradually add broth, stirring constantly until you have a smooth gravy.
8. Add garlic powder and Worcestershire sauce and simmer on low heat until sauce thickens, about 5minutes.
9. When chicken is cooked, remove baking pan from air fryer and set aside.
10. Place ham slices directly into air fryer basket and cook at 390°F for 5minutes or until hot and beginning to sizzle a little. Remove and set aside on top of the chicken for now.
11. Place the English muffin halves in air fryer basket and cook at 390°F for 1 minute.
12. Open air fryer and place a ham slice on top of each English muffin half. Stack 2 pieces of chicken on top of each ham slice. Cook at 390°F for 1 to 2minutes to heat through.
13. Place each English muffin stack on a serving plate and top with plenty of sauce.

# VEGETABLE SIDE DISHES RECIPES

## Hasselback Garlic-and-butter Potatoes

Servings: 3

Cooking Time: 48 Minutes

**Ingredients:**

- 3 8-ounce russet potatoes
- 6 Brown button or Baby Bella mushrooms, very thinly sliced
- Olive oil spray
- 3 tablespoons Butter, melted and cooled
- 1 tablespoon Minced garlic
- ¾ teaspoon Table salt
- 3 tablespoons (about ½ ounce) Finely grated Parmesan cheese

**Directions:**

1. Preheat the air fryer to 350°F .

2. Cut slits down the length of each potato, about three-quarters down into the potato and spaced about ¼ inch apart. Wedge a thin mushroom slice in each slit. Generously coat the potatoes on all sides with olive oil spray.

3. When the machine is at temperature, set the potatoes mushroom side up in the basket with as much air space between them as possible. Air-fry undisturbed for 45 minutes, or tender when pricked with a fork.

4. Increase the machine's temperature to 400°F. Use kitchen tongs, and perhaps a flatware fork for balance, to gently transfer the potatoes to a cutting board. Brush each evenly with butter, then sprinkle the minced garlic and salt over them. Sprinkle the cheese evenly over the potatoes.

5. Use those same tongs to gently transfer the potatoes cheese side up to the basket in one layer with some space for air flow between them. Air-fry undisturbed for 3 minutes, or until the cheese has melted and begun to brown.

6. Use those same tongs to gently transfer the potatoes back to the wire rack. Cool for 5 minutes before serving.

# Zucchini Fries

Servings: 3

Cooking Time: 12 Minutes

**Ingredients:**

- ➢ 1 large Zucchini
- ➢ ½ cup All-purpose flour or tapioca flour
- ➢ 2 Large egg(s), well beaten
- ➢ 1 cup Seasoned Italian-style dried bread crumbs (gluten-free, if a concern)
- ➢ Olive oil spray

**Directions:**

1. Preheat the air fryer to 400°F.

2. Trim the zucchini into a long rectangular block, taking off the ends and four "sides" to make this shape. Cut the block lengthwise into ½-inch-thick slices. Lay these slices flat and cut in half widthwise. Slice each of these pieces into ½-inch-thick batons.

3. Set up and fill three shallow soup plates or small pie plates on your counter: one for the flour, one for the beaten egg(s), and one for the bread crumbs.

4. Set a zucchini baton in the flour and turn it several times to coat all sides. Gently shake off any excess flour, then dip it in the egg(s), turning it to coat. Let any excess egg slip back into the rest, then set the baton in the bread crumbs and turn it several times, pressing gently to coat all sides, even the ends. Set aside on a cutting board and continue coating the remainder of the batons in the same way.

5. Lightly coat the batons on all sides with olive oil spray. Set them in two flat layers in the basket, the top layer at a 90-degree angle to the bottom one, with a little air space between the batons in each layer. In the end, the whole thing will look like a crosshatch pattern. Air-fry undisturbed for 6 minutes.

6. Use kitchen tongs to gently rearrange the batons so that any covered parts are now uncovered. The batons no longer need to be in a crosshatch pattern. Continue air-frying undisturbed for 6 minutes, or until lightly browned and crisp.

7. Gently pour the contents of the basket onto a wire rack. Spread the batons out and cool for only a minute or two before serving.

# Blistered Green Beans

Servings: 3

Cooking Time: 10 Minutes

**Ingredients:**

- ¾ pound Green beans, trimmed on both ends
- 1½ tablespoons Olive oil
- 3 tablespoons Pine nuts
- 1½ tablespoons Balsamic vinegar
- 1½ teaspoons Minced garlic
- ¾ teaspoon Table salt
- ¾ teaspoon Ground black pepper

**Directions:**

1. Preheat the air fryer to 400°F.

2. Toss the green beans and oil in a large bowl until all the green beans are glistening.

3. When the machine is at temperature, pile the green beans into the basket. Air-fry for 10 minutes, tossing often to rearrange the green beans in the basket, or until blistered and tender.

4. Dump the contents of the basket into a serving bowl. Add the pine nuts, vinegar, garlic, salt, and pepper. Toss well to coat and combine. Serve warm or at room temperature.

# Onion Rings

Servings: 4

Cooking Time: 12 Minutes

**Ingredients:**

- 1 large onion (preferably Vidalia or 1015)
- ½ cup flour, plus 2 tablespoons
- ½ teaspoon salt
- ½ cup beer, plus 2 tablespoons
- 1 cup crushed panko breadcrumbs
- oil for misting or cooking spray

**Directions:**

1. Peel onion, slice, and separate into rings.

2. In a large bowl, mix together the flour and salt. Add beer and stir until it stops foaming and makes a thick batter.

3. Place onion rings in batter and stir to coat.

4. Place breadcrumbs in a sealable plastic bag or container with lid.

5. Working with a few at a time, remove onion rings from batter, shaking off excess, and drop into breadcrumbs. Shake to coat, then lay out onion rings on cookie sheet or wax paper.

6. When finished, spray onion rings with oil or cooking spray and pile into air fryer basket.

7. Cook at 390°F for 5minutes. Shake basket and mist with oil. Cook 5minutes and mist again. Cook an additional 2 minutes, until golden brown and crispy.

# **Buttery Rolls**

| Servings: 6 | Cooking Time: 14 Minutes |

**Ingredients:**

- 6½ tablespoons Room-temperature whole or low-fat milk
- 3 tablespoons plus 1 teaspoon Butter, melted and cooled
- 3 tablespoons plus 1 teaspoon (or 1 medium egg, well beaten) Pasteurized egg substitute, such as Egg Beaters
- 1½ tablespoons Granulated white sugar
- 1¼ teaspoons Instant yeast
- ¼ teaspoon Table salt
- 2 cups, plus more for dusting All-purpose flour
- Vegetable oil
- Additional melted butter, for brushing

**Directions:**

1. Stir the milk, melted butter, pasteurized egg substitute (or whole egg), sugar, yeast, and salt in a medium bowl to combine. Stir in the flour just until the mixture makes a soft dough.

2. Lightly flour a clean, dry work surface. Turn the dough out onto the work surface. Knead the dough for 5 minutes to develop the gluten.

3. Lightly oil the inside of a clean medium bowl. Gather the dough into a compact ball and set it in the bowl. Turn the dough over so that its surface has oil on it all over. Cover the bowl tightly with plastic wrap and set aside in a warm, draft-free place until the dough has doubled in bulk, about 1½ hours.

4. Punch down the dough, then turn it out onto a clean, dry work surface. Divide it into 5 even balls for a small batch, 6 balls for a medium batch, or 8 balls for a large one.

5. For a small batch, lightly oil the inside of a 6-inch round cake pan and set the balls around its perimeter, separating them as much as possible.

6. For a medium batch, lightly oil the inside of a 7-inch round cake pan and set the balls in it with one ball at its center, separating them as much as possible.

7. For a large batch, lightly oil the inside of an 8-inch round cake pan and set the balls in it with one at the center, separating them as much as possible.

8. Cover with plastic wrap and set aside to rise for 30 minutes.

9. Preheat the air fryer to 350°F .

10. Uncover the pan and brush the rolls with a little melted butter, perhaps ½ teaspoon per roll. When the machine is at temperature, set the cake pan in the basket. Air-fry undisturbed for 14 minutes, or until the rolls have risen and browned.

11. Using kitchen tongs and a nonstick-safe spatula, two hot pads, or silicone baking mitts, transfer the cake pan from the basket to a wire rack. Cool the rolls in the pan for a minute or two. Turn the rolls out onto a wire rack, set them top side up again, and cool for at least another couple of minutes before serving warm.

# Sesame Carrots And Sugar Snap Peas

Servings: 4

Cooking Time: 16 Minutes

**Ingredients:**

- 1 pound carrots, peeled sliced on the bias (½-inch slices)
- 1 teaspoon olive oil
- salt and freshly ground black pepper
- ⅓ cup honey
- 1 tablespoon sesame oil
- 1 tablespoon soy sauce
- ½ teaspoon minced fresh ginger
- 4 ounces sugar snap peas (about 1 cup)
- 1½ teaspoons sesame seeds

**Directions:**

1. Preheat the air fryer to 360°F.

2. Toss the carrots with the olive oil, season with salt and pepper and air-fry for 10 minutes, shaking the basket once or twice during the cooking process.

3. Combine the honey, sesame oil, soy sauce and minced ginger in a large bowl. Add the sugar snap peas and the air-fried carrots to the honey mixture, toss to coat and return everything to the air fryer basket.

4. Turn up the temperature to 400°F and air-fry for an additional 6 minutes, shaking the basket once during the cooking process.

5. Transfer the carrots and sugar snap peas to a serving bowl. Pour the sauce from the bottom of the cooker over the vegetables and sprinkle sesame seeds over top. Serve immediately.

# Wilted Brussels Sprout Slaw

Servings: 4

Cooking Time: 18 Minutes

**Ingredients:**

- 2 Thick-cut bacon strip(s), halved widthwise (gluten-free, if a concern)
- 4½ cups (about 1 pound 2 ounces) Bagged shredded Brussels sprouts
- ¼ teaspoon Table salt
- 2 tablespoons White balsamic vinegar (see here)
- 2 teaspoons Worcestershire sauce (gluten-free, if a concern)
- 1 teaspoon Dijon mustard (gluten-free, if a concern)
- ¼ teaspoon Ground black pepper

**Directions:**

1. Preheat the air fryer to 375°F .

2. When the machine is at temperature, lay the bacon strip halves in the basket in one layer and air-fry for 10 minutes, or until crisp.

3. Use kitchen tongs to transfer the bacon pieces to a wire rack. Put the shredded Brussels sprouts in a large bowl. Drain any fat from the basket or the tray under the basket onto the Brussels sprouts. Add the salt and toss well to coat.

4. Put the Brussels sprout shreds in the basket, spreading them out into as close to an even layer as you can. Air-fry for 8 minutes, tossing the basket's contents at least three times, until wilted and lightly browned.

5. Pour the contents of the basket into a serving bowl. Chop the bacon and add it to the Brussels sprouts. Add the vinegar, Worcestershire sauce, mustard, and pepper. Toss well to blend the dressing and coat the Brussels sprout shreds. Serve warm.

# **Sweet Potato Fries**

Servings: 4

Cooking Time: 30 Minutes

**Ingredients:**

- ➢ 2 pounds sweet potatoes
- ➢ 1 teaspoon dried marjoram
- ➢ 2 teaspoons olive oil
- ➢ sea salt

**Directions:**

1. Peel and cut the potatoes into ¼-inch sticks, 4 to 5 inches long.

2. In a sealable plastic bag or bowl with lid, toss sweet potatoes with marjoram and olive oil. Rub seasonings in to coat well.

3. Pour sweet potatoes into air fryer basket and cook at 390°F for approximately 30 minutes, until cooked through with some brown spots on edges.

4. Season to taste with sea salt.

# Tandoori Cauliflower

Servings: 4

Cooking Time: 10 Minutes

**Ingredients:**

- ½ cup Plain full-fat yogurt (not Greek yogurt)
- 1½ teaspoons Yellow curry powder, purchased or homemade (see the headnote)
- 1½ teaspoons Lemon juice
- ¾ teaspoon Table salt (optional)
- 4½ cups (about 1 pound 2 ounces) 2-inch cauliflower florets

**Directions:**

1. Preheat the air fryer to 400°F.

2. Whisk the yogurt, curry powder, lemon juice, and salt (if using) in a large bowl until uniform. Add the florets and stir gently to coat the florets well and evenly. Even better, use your clean, dry hands to get the yogurt mixture down into all the nooks of the florets.

3. When the machine is at temperature, transfer the florets to the basket, spreading them gently into as close to one layer as you can. Air-fry for 10 minutes, tossing and rearranging the florets twice so that any covered or touching parts are exposed to the air currents, until lightly browned and tender if still a bit crunchy.

4. Pour the contents of the basket onto a wire rack. Cool for at least 5 minutes before serving, or serve at room temperature.

# Homemade Potato Puffs

Servings: 4

Cooking Time: 15 Minutes

**Ingredients:**

- 1¾ cups Water
- 4 tablespoons (¼ cup/½ stick) Butter
- 2 cups plus 2 tablespoons Instant mashed potato flakes
- 1½ teaspoons Table salt
- ¾ teaspoon Ground black pepper
- ¼ teaspoon Mild paprika
- ¼ teaspoon Dried thyme
- 1¼ cups Seasoned Italian-style dried bread crumbs (gluten-free, if a concern)
- Olive oil spray

**Directions:**

1. Heat the water with the butter in a medium saucepan set over medium-low heat just until the butter melts. Do not bring to a boil.

2. Remove the saucepan from the heat and stir in the potato flakes, salt, pepper, paprika, and thyme until smooth. Set aside to cool for 5 minutes.

3. Preheat the air fryer to 400°F. Spread the bread crumbs on a dinner plate.

4. Scrape up 2 tablespoons of the potato flake mixture and form it into a small, oblong puff, like a little cylinder about 1½ inches long. Gently roll the puff in the bread crumbs until coated on all sides. Set it aside and continue making more, about 12 for the small batch, 18 for the medium batch, or 24 for the large.

5. Coat the potato cylinders with olive oil spray on all sides, then arrange them in the basket in one layer with some air space between them. Air-fry undisturbed for 15 minutes, or until crisp and brown.

6. Gently dump the contents of the basket onto a wire rack. Cool for 5 minutes before serving.

# Perfect Broccoli

Servings: 4

Cooking Time: 12 Minutes

**Ingredients:**

- 5 cups (about 1 pound 10 ounces) 1- to 1½-inch fresh broccoli florets (not frozen)
- Olive oil spray
- ¾ teaspoon Table salt

**Directions:**

1.  Preheat the air fryer to 375°F .

2.  Put the broccoli florets in a big bowl, coat them generously with olive oil spray, then toss to coat all surfaces, even down into the crannies, spraying them in a couple of times more. Sprinkle the salt on top and toss again.

3.  When the machine is at temperature, pour the florets into the basket. Air-fry for 10 minutes, tossing and rearranging the pieces twice so that all the covered or touching bits are eventually exposed to the air currents, until lightly browned but still crunchy. (If the machine is at 360°F, you may have to add 2 minutes to the cooking time.)

4.  Pour the florets into a serving bowl. Cool for a minute or two, then serve hot.

# Broccoli Tots

Servings: 24

Cooking Time: 10 Minutes

**Ingredients:**

- ➤ 2 cups broccoli florets (about ½ pound broccoli crowns)
- ➤ 1 egg, beaten
- ➤ ⅛ teaspoon onion powder
- ➤ ¼ teaspoon salt
- ➤ ⅛ teaspoon pepper
- ➤ 2 tablespoons grated Parmesan cheese
- ➤ ¼ cup panko breadcrumbs
- ➤ oil for misting

**Directions:**

1. Steam broccoli for 2minutes. Rinse in cold water, drain well, and chop finely.
2. In a large bowl, mix broccoli with all other ingredients except the oil.
3. Scoop out small portions of mixture and shape into 24 tots. Lay them on a cookie sheet or wax paper as you work.
4. Spray tots with oil and place in air fryer basket in single layer.
5. Cook at 390°F for 5minutes. Shake basket and spray with oil again. Cook 5minutes longer or until browned and crispy.

# BEEF , PORK & LAMB RECIPES

## Steak Fingers

Servings: 4

Cooking Time: 8 Minutes

**Ingredients:**

- 4 small beef cube steaks
- salt and pepper
- ½ cup flour
- oil for misting or cooking spray

**Directions:**

1. Cut cube steaks into 1-inch-wide strips.
2. Sprinkle lightly with salt and pepper to taste.
3. Roll in flour to coat all sides.
4. Spray air fryer basket with cooking spray or oil.
5. Place steak strips in air fryer basket in single layer, very close together but not touching. Spray top of steak strips with oil or cooking spray.
6. Cook at 390°F for 4minutes, turn strips over, and spray with oil or cooking spray.
7. Cook 4 more minutes and test with fork for doneness. Steak fingers should be crispy outside with no red juices inside. If needed, cook an additional 4 minutes or until well done. (Don't eat beef cube steak rare.)
8. Repeat steps 5 through 7 to cook remaining strips.

# Albóndigas

Servings: 4

Cooking Time: 15 Minutes

**Ingredients:**

- ➢ 1 pound Lean ground pork
- ➢ 3 tablespoons Very finely chopped trimmed scallions
- ➢ 3 tablespoons Finely chopped fresh cilantro leaves
- ➢ 3 tablespoons Plain panko bread crumbs (gluten-free, if a concern)
- ➢ 3 tablespoons Dry white wine, dry sherry, or unsweetened apple juice
- ➢ 1½ teaspoons Minced garlic
- ➢ 1¼ teaspoons Mild smoked paprika
- ➢ ¾ teaspoon Dried oregano
- ➢ ¾ teaspoon Table salt
- ➢ ¼ teaspoon Ground black pepper
- ➢ Olive oil spray

**Directions:**

1. Preheat the air fryer to 400°F.

2. Mix the ground pork, scallions, cilantro, bread crumbs, wine or its substitute, garlic, smoked paprika, oregano, salt, and pepper in a bowl until the herbs and spices are evenly distributed in the mixture.

3. Lightly coat your clean hands with olive oil spray, then form the ground pork mixture into balls, using 2 tablespoons for each one. Spray your hands frequently so that the meat mixture doesn't stick.

4. Set the balls in the basket so that they're not touching, even if they're close together. Air-fry undisturbed for 15 minutes, or until well browned and an instant-read meat thermometer inserted into one or two balls registers 165°F.

5. Use a nonstick-safe spatula and kitchen tongs for balance to gently transfer the fragile balls to a wire rack to cool for 5 minutes before serving.

# Crispy Pork Medallions With Radicchio And Endive Salad

Servings: 4          Cooking Time: 7 Minutes

**Ingredients:**

- 1 (8-ounce) pork tenderloin
- salt and freshly ground black pepper
- ¼ cup flour
- 2 eggs, lightly beaten
- ¾ cup cracker meal
- 1 teaspoon paprika
- 1 teaspoon dry mustard
- 1 teaspoon garlic powder
- 1 teaspoon dried thyme
- 1 teaspoon salt
- vegetable or canola oil, in spray bottle
- Vinaigrette
- ¼ cup white balsamic vinegar
- 2 tablespoons agave syrup (or honey or maple syrup)
- 1 tablespoon Dijon mustard
- juice of ½ lemon
- 2 tablespoons chopped chervil or flat-leaf parsley
- salt and freshly ground black pepper
- ½ cup extra-virgin olive oil
- Radicchio and Endive Salad
- 1 heart romaine lettuce, torn into large pieces
- ½ head radicchio, coarsely chopped
- 2 heads endive, sliced
- ½ cup cherry tomatoes, halved
- 3 ounces fresh mozzarella, diced
- salt and freshly ground black pepper

**Directions:**

1. Slice the pork tenderloin into 1-inch slices. Using a meat pounder, pound the pork slices into thin ½-inch medallions. Generously season the pork with salt and freshly ground black pepper on both sides.

2. Set up a dredging station using three shallow dishes. Place the flour in one dish and the beaten eggs in a second dish. Combine the cracker meal, paprika, dry mustard, garlic powder, thyme and salt in a third dish.

3. Preheat the air fryer to 400°F.

4. Dredge the pork medallions in flour first and then into the beaten egg. Let the excess egg drip off and coat both sides of the medallions with the cracker meal crumb mixture. Spray both sides of the coated medallions with vegetable or canola oil.

5. Air-fry the medallions in two batches at 400°F for 5 minutes. Once you have air-fried all the medallions, flip them all over and return the first batch of medallions back into the air fryer on top of the second batch. Air-fry at 400°F for an additional 2 minutes.

6.  While the medallions are cooking, make the salad and dressing. Whisk the white balsamic vinegar, agave syrup, Dijon mustard, lemon juice, chervil, salt and pepper together in a small bowl. Whisk in the olive oil slowly until combined and thickened.

7.  Combine the romaine lettuce, radicchio, endive, cherry tomatoes, and mozzarella cheese in a large salad bowl. Drizzle the dressing over the vegetables and toss to combine. Season with salt and freshly ground black pepper.

8.  Serve the pork medallions warm on or beside the salad.

# Teriyaki Country-style Pork Ribs

Servings: 3

Cooking Time: 30 Minutes

**Ingredients:**

- ➢ 3 tablespoons Regular or low-sodium soy sauce or gluten-free tamari sauce
- ➢ 3 tablespoons Honey
- ➢ ¾ teaspoon Ground dried ginger
- ➢ ¾ teaspoon Garlic powder
- ➢ 3 8-ounce boneless country-style pork ribs
- ➢ Vegetable oil spray

**Directions:**

1.  Preheat the air fryer to 350°F .

2.  Mix the soy or tamari sauce, honey, ground ginger, and garlic powder in another bowl until uniform.

3.  Smear about half of this teriyaki sauce over all sides of the country-style ribs. Reserve the remainder of the teriyaki sauce. Generously coat the meat with vegetable oil spray.

4.  When the machine is at temperature, place the country-style ribs in the basket with as much air space between them as possible. Air-fry undisturbed for 15 minutes. Turn the country-style ribs (but keep the space between them) and brush them all over with the remaining teriyaki sauce. Continue air-frying undisturbed for 15 minutes, or until an instant-read meat thermometer inserted into the center of one rib registers at least 145°F.

5.  Use kitchen tongs to transfer the country-style ribs to a wire rack. Cool for 5 minutes before serving.

# Flank Steak With Roasted Peppers And Chimichurri



**Ingredients:**

- 2 cups flat-leaf parsley leaves
- ¼ cup fresh oregano leaves
- 3 cloves garlic
- ½ cup olive oil
- ¼ cup red wine vinegar
- ½ teaspoon salt
- freshly ground black pepper
- ¼ teaspoon crushed red pepper flakes
- ½ teaspoon ground cumin
- 1 pound flank steak
- 1 red bell pepper, cut into strips
- 1 yellow bell pepper, cut into strips

**Directions:**

1. Make the chimichurri sauce by chopping the parsley, oregano and garlic in a food processor. Add the olive oil, vinegar and seasonings and process again. Pour half of the sauce into a shallow dish with the flank steak and set the remaining sauce aside. Pierce the flank steak with a needle-style meat tenderizer or a paring knife and marinate the steak for 2 to 24 hours in the refrigerator. When you are ready to cook, remove the steak from the refrigerator and let it sit at room temperature for 30 minutes.

2. Preheat the air fryer to 400°F.

3. Cut the flank steak in half so that it fits more easily into the air fryer and transfer both pieces to the air fryer basket. Air-fry for 14 minutes, depending on how you like your steak cooked (10 minutes will give you medium for a 1-inch thick flank steak). Flip the steak over halfway through the cooking time.

4. When the flank steak is cooked to your liking, transfer it to a cutting board, loosely tent with foil and let it rest while you cook the peppers.

5. Toss the peppers in a little olive oil, salt and freshly ground black pepper and transfer them to the air fryer basket. Air-fry at 400°F for 8 minutes, shaking the basket once or twice throughout the cooking process. To serve, slice the flank steak against the grain of the meat and top with the roasted peppers. Drizzle the reserved chimichurri sauce on top, thinning the sauce with another tablespoon of olive oil if desired.

# Cinnamon-stick Kofta Skewers

Servings: 8

Cooking Time: 15 Minutes

**Ingredients:**

- ➢ 1 pound Lean ground beef
- ➢ ½ teaspoon Ground cumin
- ➢ ½ teaspoon Onion powder
- ➢ ½ teaspoon Ground dried turmeric
- ➢ ½ teaspoon Ground cinnamon
- ➢ ½ teaspoon Table salt
- ➢ Up to a ⅛ teaspoon Cayenne
- ➢ 8 3½- to 4-inch-long cinnamon sticks (see the headnote)
- ➢ Vegetable oil spray

**Directions:**

1. Preheat the air fryer to 375°F .

2. Gently mix the ground beef, cumin, onion powder, turmeric, cinnamon, salt, and cayenne in a bowl until the meat is evenly mixed with the spices. (Clean, dry hands work best!) Divide this mixture into 2-ounce portions, each about the size of a golf ball.

3. Wrap one portion of the meat mixture around a cinnamon stick, using about three-quarters of the length of the stick, covering one end but leaving a little "handle" of cinnamon stick protruding from the other end. Set aside and continue making more kofta skewers.

4. Generously coat the formed kofta skewers on all sides with vegetable oil spray. Set them in the basket with as much air space between them as possible. Air-fry undisturbed for 13 minutes, or until browned and cooked through. If the machine is at 360°F, you may need to add 2 minutes to the cooking time.

5. Use a nonstick-safe spatula, and perhaps kitchen tongs for balance, to gently transfer the kofta skewers to a wire rack. Cool for at least 5 minutes or up to 20 minutes before serving.

# Easy Carnitas

Servings: 3

Cooking Time: 25 Minutes

**Ingredients:**

- 1½ pounds Boneless country-style pork ribs, cut into 2-inch pieces
- ¼ cup Orange juice
- 2 tablespoons Brine from a jar of pickles, any type, even pickled jalapeño rings (gluten-free, if a concern)
- 2 teaspoons Minced garlic
- 2 teaspoons Minced fresh oregano leaves
- ¾ teaspoon Ground cumin
- ¾ teaspoon Table salt
- ¾ teaspoon Ground black pepper

**Directions:**

1. Mix the country-style pork rib pieces, orange juice, pickle brine, garlic, oregano, cumin, salt, and pepper in a large bowl. Cover and refrigerate for at least 2 hours or up to 10 hours, stirring the mixture occasionally.

2. Preheat the air fryer to 400°F. Set the rib pieces in their bowl on the counter as the machine heats.

3. Use kitchen tongs to transfer the rib pieces to the basket, arranging them in one layer. Some may touch. Air-fry for 25 minutes, turning and rearranging the pieces at the 10- and 20-minute marks to make sure all surfaces have been exposed to the air currents, until browned and sizzling.

4. Use clean kitchen tongs to transfer the rib pieces to a wire rack. Cool for a couple of minutes before serving.

# Zesty London Broil

Servings: 4

Cooking Time: 28 Minutes

**Ingredients:**

- ⅔ cup ketchup
- ¼ cup honey
- ¼ cup olive oil
- 2 tablespoons apple cider vinegar
- 2 tablespoons Worcestershire sauce
- 2 tablespoons minced onion
- ½ teaspoon paprika
- 1 teaspoon salt
- 1 teaspoon freshly ground black pepper
- 2 pounds London broil, top round or flank steak (about 1-inch thick)

**Directions:**

1. Combine the ketchup, honey, olive oil, apple cider vinegar, Worcestershire sauce, minced onion, paprika, salt and pepper in a small bowl and whisk together.

2. Generously pierce both sides of the meat with a fork or meat tenderizer and place it in a shallow dish. Pour the marinade mixture over the steak, making sure all sides of the meat get coated with the marinade. Cover and refrigerate overnight.

3. Preheat the air fryer to 400°F.

4. Transfer the London broil to the air fryer basket and air-fry for 28 minutes, depending on how rare or well done you like your steak. Flip the steak over halfway through the cooking time.

5. Remove the London broil from the air fryer and let it rest for five minutes on a cutting board. To serve, thinly slice the meat against the grain and transfer to a serving platter.

# Skirt Steak Fajitas

Servings: 4                                   Cooking Time: 30 Minutes

**Ingredients:**

- 2 tablespoons olive oil
- ¼ cup lime juice
- 1 clove garlic, minced
- ½ teaspoon ground cumin
- ½ teaspoon hot sauce
- ½ teaspoon salt
- 2 tablespoons chopped fresh cilantro
- 1 pound skirt steak
- 1 onion, sliced

- 1 teaspoon chili powder
- 1 red pepper, sliced
- 1 green pepper, sliced
- salt and freshly ground black pepper
- 8 flour tortillas
- shredded lettuce, crumbled Queso Fresco (or grated Cheddar cheese), sliced black olives, diced tomatoes, sour cream and guacamole for serving

**Directions:**

1.  Combine the olive oil, lime juice, garlic, cumin, hot sauce, salt and cilantro in a shallow dish. Add the skirt steak and turn it over several times to coat all sides. Pierce the steak with a needle-style meat tenderizer or paring knife. Marinate the steak in the refrigerator for at least 3 hours, or overnight. When you are ready to cook, remove the steak from the refrigerator and let it sit at room temperature for 30 minutes.

2.  Preheat the air fryer to 400°F.

3.  Toss the onion slices with the chili powder and a little olive oil and transfer them to the air fryer basket. Air-fry at 400°F for 5 minutes. Add the red and green peppers to the air fryer basket with the onions, season with salt and pepper and air-fry for 8 more minutes, until the onions and peppers are soft. Transfer the vegetables to a dish and cover with aluminum foil to keep warm.

4.  Place the skirt steak in the air fryer basket and pour the marinade over the top. Air-fry at 400°F for 12 minutes. Flip the steak over and air-fry at 400°F for an additional 5 minutes. (The time needed for your steak will depend on the thickness of the skirt steak. 17 minutes should bring your steak to roughly medium.) Transfer the cooked steak to a cutting board and let the steak rest for a few minutes. If the peppers and onions need to be heated, return them to the air fryer for just 1 to 2 minutes.

5.  Thinly slice the steak at an angle, cutting against the grain of the steak. Serve the steak with the onions and peppers, the warm tortillas and the fajita toppings on the side so that everyone can make their own fajita.

# Crispy Pierogi With Kielbasa And Onions

Servings: 3

Cooking Time: 20 Minutes

**Ingredients:**

- ➢ 6 Frozen potato and cheese pierogi, thawed (about 12 pierogi to 1 pound)
- ➢ ½ pound Smoked kielbasa, sliced into ½-inch-thick rounds
- ➢ ¾ cup Very roughly chopped sweet onion, preferably Vidalia
- ➢ Vegetable oil spray

**Directions:**

1. Preheat the air fryer to 375°F .

2. Put the pierogi, kielbasa rounds, and onion in a large bowl. Coat them with vegetable oil spray, toss well, spray again, and toss until everything is glistening.

3. When the machine is at temperature, dump the contents of the bowl it into the basket. (Items may be leaning against each other and even on top of each other.) Air-fry, tossing and rearranging everything twice so that all covered surfaces get exposed, for 20 minutes, or until the sausages have begun to brown and the pierogi are crisp.

4. Pour the contents of the basket onto a serving platter. Wait a minute or two just to take make sure nothing's searing hot before serving.

# City "chicken"

Servings: 3

Cooking Time: 10 Minutes

**Ingredients:**

- ➢ 1 pound Pork tenderloin, cut into 2-inch cubes
- ➢ ½ cup All-purpose flour or tapioca flour
- ➢ 1 Large egg(s)
- ➢ 1 teaspoon Dried poultry seasoning blend
- ➢ 1¼ cups Plain panko bread crumbs (gluten-free, if a concern)
- ➢ Vegetable oil spray

**Directions:**

1. Preheat the air fryer to 350°F .

2. Thread 3 or 4 pieces of pork on a 4-inch bamboo skewer. You'll need 2 or 3 skewers for a small batch, 3 or 4 for a medium, and up to 6 for a large batch.

3. Set up and fill three shallow soup plates or small pie plates on your counter: one for the flour; one for the egg(s), beaten with the poultry seasoning until foamy; and one for the bread crumbs.

4. Dip and roll one skewer into the flour, coating all sides of the meat. Gently shake off any excess flour, then dip and roll the skewer in the egg mixture. Let any excess egg mixture slip back into the rest, then set the skewer in the bread crumbs and roll it around, pressing gently, until the exterior surfaces of the meat are evenly coated. Generously coat the meat on the skewer with vegetable oil spray. Set aside and continue dredging, dipping, coating, and spraying the remaining skewers.

5. Set the skewers in the basket in one layer and air-fry undisturbed for 10 minutes, or until brown and crunchy.

6. Use kitchen tongs to transfer the skewers to a wire rack. Cool for a minute or two before serving.

# Easy Tex-mex Chimichangas

Servings: 2

Cooking Time: 8 Minutes

**Ingredients:**

- ¼ pound Thinly sliced deli roast beef, chopped
- ½ cup (about 2 ounces) Shredded Cheddar cheese or shredded Tex-Mex cheese blend
- ¼ cup Jarred salsa verde or salsa rojo
- ½ teaspoon Ground cumin
- ½ teaspoon Dried oregano
- 2 Burrito-size (12-inch) flour tortilla(s), not corn tortillas (gluten-free, if a concern)
- ⅔ cup Canned refried beans
- Vegetable oil spray

**Directions:**

1. Preheat the air fryer to 375°F .
2. Stir the roast beef, cheese, salsa, cumin, and oregano in a bowl until well mixed.
3. Lay a tortilla on a clean, dry work surface. Spread ⅓ cup of the refried beans in the center lower third of the tortilla(s), leaving an inch on either side of the spread beans.
4. For one chimichanga, spread all of the roast beef mixture on top of the beans. For two, spread half of the roast beef mixture on each tortilla.
5. At either "end" of the filling mixture, fold the sides of the tortilla up and over the filling, partially covering it. Starting with the unfolded side of the tortilla just below the filling, roll the tortilla closed. Fold and roll the second filled tortilla, as necessary.
6. Coat the exterior of the tortilla(s) with vegetable oil spray. Set the chimichanga(s) seam side down in the basket, with at least ½ inch air space between them if you're working with two. Air-fry undisturbed for 8 minutes, or until the tortilla is lightly browned and crisp.
7. Use kitchen tongs to gently transfer the chimichanga(s) to a wire rack. Cool for at last 5 minutes or up to 20 minutes before serving.

# BREAD AND BREAKFAST

## Sweet-hot Pepperoni Pizza

Servings: 2

Cooking Time: 18 Minutes

**Ingredients:**

- 1 (6- to 8-ounce) pizza dough ball*
- olive oil
- ½ cup pizza sauce
- ¾ cup grated mozzarella cheese
- ½ cup thick sliced pepperoni
- ⅓ cup sliced pickled hot banana peppers
- ¼ teaspoon dried oregano
- 2 teaspoons honey

**Directions:**

1. Preheat the air fryer to 390°F.

2. Cut out a piece of aluminum foil the same size as the bottom of the air fryer basket. Brush the foil circle with olive oil. Shape the dough into a circle and place it on top of the foil. Dock the dough by piercing it several times with a fork. Brush the dough lightly with olive oil and transfer it into the air fryer basket with the foil on the bottom.

3. Air-fry the plain pizza dough for 6 minutes. Turn the dough over, remove the aluminum foil and brush again with olive oil. Air-fry for an additional 4 minutes.

4. Spread the pizza sauce on top of the dough and sprinkle the mozzarella cheese over the sauce. Top with the pepperoni, pepper slices and dried oregano. Lower the temperature of the air fryer to 350°F and cook for 8 minutes, until the cheese has melted and lightly browned. Transfer the pizza to a cutting board and drizzle with the honey. Slice and serve.

# Orange Rolls

Servings: 8                                          Cooking Time: 10 Minutes

**Ingredients:**

- parchment paper
- 3 ounces low-fat cream cheese
- 1 tablespoon low-fat sour cream or plain yogurt (not Greek yogurt)
- 2 teaspoons sugar
- ¼ teaspoon pure vanilla extract
- ¼ teaspoon orange extract
- 1 can (8 count) organic crescent roll dough
- ¼ cup chopped walnuts
- ¼ cup dried cranberries
- ¼ cup shredded, sweetened coconut
- butter-flavored cooking spray
- Orange Glaze
- ½ cup powdered sugar
- 1 tablespoon orange juice
- ¼ teaspoon orange extract
- dash of salt

**Directions:**

1. Cut a circular piece of parchment paper slightly smaller than the bottom of your air fryer basket. Set aside.

2. In a small bowl, combine the cream cheese, sour cream or yogurt, sugar, and vanilla and orange extracts. Stir until smooth.

3. Preheat air fryer to 300°F.

4. Separate crescent roll dough into 8 triangles and divide cream cheese mixture among them. Starting at wide end, spread cheese mixture to within 1 inch of point.

5. Sprinkle nuts and cranberries evenly over cheese mixture.

6. Starting at wide end, roll up triangles, then sprinkle with coconut, pressing in lightly to make it stick. Spray tops of rolls with butter-flavored cooking spray.

7. Place parchment paper in air fryer basket, and place 4 rolls on top, spaced evenly.

8. Cook for 10minutes, until rolls are golden brown and cooked through.

9. Repeat steps 7 and 8 to cook remaining 4 rolls. You should be able to use the same piece of parchment paper twice.

10. In a small bowl, stir together ingredients for glaze and drizzle over warm rolls.

# Western Omelet

Servings: 2

Cooking Time: 22 Minutes

**Ingredients:**

- ¼ cup chopped onion
- ¼ cup chopped bell pepper, green or red
- ¼ cup diced ham
- 1 teaspoon butter
- 4 large eggs
- 2 tablespoons milk
- ⅛ teaspoon salt
- ¾ cup grated sharp Cheddar cheese

**Directions:**

1. Place onion, bell pepper, ham, and butter in air fryer baking pan. Cook at 390°F for 1 minute and stir. Continue cooking 5minutes, until vegetables are tender.

2. Beat together eggs, milk, and salt. Pour over vegetables and ham in baking pan. Cook at 360°F for 15minutes or until eggs set and top has browned slightly.

3. Sprinkle grated cheese on top of omelet. Cook 1 minute or just long enough to melt the cheese.

# **Strawberry Toast**

Servings: 4

Cooking Time: 8 Minutes

**Ingredients:**

- ➢ 4 slices bread, ½-inch thick
- ➢ butter-flavored cooking spray
- ➢ 1 cup sliced strawberries
- ➢ 1 teaspoon sugar

**Directions:**

1. Spray one side of each bread slice with butter-flavored cooking spray. Lay slices sprayed side down.
2. Divide the strawberries among the bread slices.
3. Sprinkle evenly with the sugar and place in the air fryer basket in a single layer.
4. Cook at 390°F for 8minutes. The bottom should look brown and crisp and the top should look glazed.

# Carrot Orange Muffins

Servings: 12

Cooking Time: 12 Minutes

**Ingredients:**

- 1½ cups all-purpose flour
- ½ cup granulated sugar
- ½ teaspoon ground cinnamon
- 2 teaspoons baking powder
- ¼ teaspoon baking soda
- ½ teaspoon salt
- 2 large eggs
- ¼ cup vegetable oil
- ⅓ cup orange marmalade
- 2 cups grated carrots

**Directions:**

1. Preheat the air fryer to 320°F.

2. In a large bowl, whisk together the flour, sugar, cinnamon, baking powder, baking soda, and salt; set aside.

3. In a separate bowl, whisk together the eggs, vegetable oil, orange marmalade, and grated carrots.

4. Make a well in the dry ingredients; then pour the wet ingredients into the well of the dry ingredients. Using a rubber spatula, mix the ingredients for 1 minute or until slightly lumpy.

5. Using silicone muffin liners, fill 6 muffin liners two-thirds full.

6. Carefully place the muffin liners in the air fryer basket and bake for 12 minutes (or until the tops are browned and a toothpick inserted in the center comes out clean). Carefully remove the muffins from the basket and repeat with remaining batter.

7. Serve warm.

# Apple-cinnamon-walnut Muffins

Servings: 8

Cooking Time: 11 Minutes

**Ingredients:**

- 1 cup flour
- ⅓ cup sugar
- 1 teaspoon baking powder
- ¼ teaspoon baking soda
- ¼ teaspoon salt
- 1 teaspoon cinnamon
- ¼ teaspoon ginger
- ¼ teaspoon nutmeg
- 1 egg
- 2 tablespoons pancake syrup, plus 2 teaspoons
- 2 tablespoons melted butter, plus 2 teaspoons
- ¾ cup unsweetened applesauce
- ½ teaspoon vanilla extract
- ¼ cup chopped walnuts
- ¼ cup diced apple
- 8 foil muffin cups, liners removed and sprayed with cooking spray

**Directions:**

1. Preheat air fryer to 330°F.
2. In a large bowl, stir together flour, sugar, baking powder, baking soda, salt, cinnamon, ginger, and nutmeg.
3. In a small bowl, beat egg until frothy. Add syrup, butter, applesauce, and vanilla and mix well.
4. Pour egg mixture into dry ingredients and stir just until moistened.
5. Gently stir in nuts and diced apple.
6. Divide batter among the 8 muffin cups.
7. Place 4 muffin cups in air fryer basket and cook at 330°F for 11minutes.
8. Repeat with remaining 4 muffins or until toothpick inserted in center comes out clean.

# Garlic Parmesan Bread Ring

Servings: 6                                                       Cooking Time: 30 Minutes

**Ingredients:**

- ½ cup unsalted butter, melted
- ¼ teaspoon salt (omit if using salted butter)
- ¾ cup grated Parmesan cheese
- 3 to 4 cloves garlic, minced
- 1 tablespoon chopped fresh parsley
- 1 pound frozen bread dough, defrosted
- olive oil
- 1 egg, beaten

**Directions:**

1. Combine the melted butter, salt, Parmesan cheese, garlic and chopped parsley in a small bowl.

2. Roll the dough out into a rectangle that measures 8 inches by 17 inches. Spread the butter mixture over the dough, leaving a half-inch border un-buttered along one of the long edges. Roll the dough from one long edge to the other, ending with the un-buttered border. Pinch the seam shut tightly. Shape the log into a circle sealing the ends together by pushing one end into the other and stretching the dough around it.

3. Cut out a circle of aluminum foil that is the same size as the air fryer basket. Brush the foil circle with oil and place an oven safe ramekin or glass in the center. Transfer the dough ring to the aluminum foil circle, around the ramekin. This will help you make sure the dough will fit in the basket and maintain its ring shape. Use kitchen shears to cut 8 slits around the outer edge of the dough ring halfway to the center. Brush the dough ring with egg wash.

4. Preheat the air fryer to 400°F for 4 minutes. When it has Preheated, brush the sides of the basket with oil and transfer the dough ring, foil circle and ramekin into the basket. Slide the drawer back into the air fryer, but do not turn the air fryer on. Let the dough rise inside the warm air fryer for 30 minutes.

5. After the bread has proofed in the air fryer for 30 minutes, set the temperature to 340°F and air-fry the bread ring for 15 minutes. Flip the bread over by inverting it onto a plate or cutting board and sliding it back into the air fryer basket. Air-fry for another 15 minutes. Let the bread cool for a few minutes before slicing the bread ring in between the slits and serving warm.

# Nutty Whole Wheat Muffins

Servings: 8 | Cooking Time: 11 Minutes

**Ingredients:**

- ½ cup whole-wheat flour, plus 2 tablespoons
- ¼ cup oat bran
- 2 tablespoons flaxseed meal
- ¼ cup brown sugar
- ½ teaspoon baking soda
- ½ teaspoon baking powder
- ¼ teaspoon salt
- ½ teaspoon cinnamon
- ½ cup buttermilk
- 2 tablespoons melted butter
- 1 egg
- ½ teaspoon pure vanilla extract
- ½ cup grated carrots
- ¼ cup chopped pecans
- ¼ cup chopped walnuts
- 1 tablespoon pumpkin seeds
- 1 tablespoon sunflower seeds
- 16 foil muffin cups, paper liners removed
- cooking spray

**Directions:**

1. Preheat air fryer to 330°F.
2. In a large bowl, stir together the flour, bran, flaxseed meal, sugar, baking soda, baking powder, salt, and cinnamon.
3. In a medium bowl, beat together the buttermilk, butter, egg, and vanilla. Pour into flour mixture and stir just until dry ingredients moisten. Do not beat.
4. Gently stir in carrots, nuts, and seeds.
5. Double up the foil cups so you have 8 total and spray with cooking spray.
6. Place 4 foil cups in air fryer basket and divide half the batter among them.
7. Cook at 330°F for 11minutes or until toothpick inserted in center comes out clean.
8. Repeat step 7 to cook remaining 4 muffins.

# Roasted Vegetable Frittata

Servings: 1

Cooking Time: 19 Minutes

**Ingredients:**

- ½ red or green bell pepper, cut into ½-inch chunks
- 4 button mushrooms, sliced
- ½ cup diced zucchini
- ½ teaspoon chopped fresh oregano or thyme
- 1 teaspoon olive oil
- 3 eggs, beaten
- ½ cup grated Cheddar cheese
- salt and freshly ground black pepper, to taste
- 1 teaspoon butter
- 1 teaspoon chopped fresh parsley

**Directions:**

1. Preheat the air fryer to 400°F.

2. Toss the peppers, mushrooms, zucchini and oregano with the olive oil and air-fry for 6 minutes, shaking the basket once or twice during the cooking process to redistribute the ingredients.

3. While the vegetables are cooking, beat the eggs well in a bowl, stir in the Cheddar cheese and season with salt and freshly ground black pepper. Add the air-fried vegetables to this bowl when they have finished cooking.

4. Place a 6- or 7-inch non-stick metal cake pan into the air fryer basket with the butter using an aluminum sling to lower the pan into the basket. (Fold a piece of aluminum foil into a strip about 2-inches wide by 24-inches long.) Air-fry for 1 minute at 380°F to melt the butter. Remove the cake pan and rotate the pan to distribute the butter and grease the pan. Pour the egg mixture into the cake pan and return the pan to the air fryer, using the aluminum sling.

5. Air-fry at 380°F for 12 minutes, or until the frittata has puffed up and is lightly browned. Let the frittata sit in the air fryer for 5 minutes to cool to an edible temperature and set up. Remove the cake pan from the air fryer, sprinkle with parsley and serve immediately.

# Strawberry Streusel Muffins

Servings: 12          Cooking Time: 14 Minutes

**Ingredients:**

- 1¾ cups all-purpose flour
- ½ cup granulated sugar
- 2 teaspoons baking powder
- ¼ teaspoon baking soda
- ½ teaspoon salt
- ½ cup plain yogurt
- ½ cup milk
- ¼ cup vegetable oil
- 2 large eggs
- 1 teaspoon vanilla extract
- ½ cup freeze-dried strawberries
- 2 tablespoons brown sugar
- ¼ cup oats
- 2 tablespoons butter

**Directions:**

1. Preheat the air fryer to 330°F.

2. In a large bowl, whisk together the flour, sugar, baking powder, baking soda, and salt; set aside.

3. In a separate bowl, whisk together the yogurt, milk, vegetable oil, eggs, and vanilla extract.

4. Make a well in the dry ingredients; then pour the wet ingredients into the well of the dry ingredients. Using a rubber spatula, mix the ingredients for 1 minute or until slightly lumpy. Fold in the strawberries.

5. In a small bowl, use your fingers to mix together the brown sugar, oats, and butter until coarse crumbles appear. Divide the mixture in half.

6. Using silicone muffin liners, fill 6 muffin liners two-thirds full.

7. Crumble half of the streusel topping onto the first batch of muffins.

8. Carefully place the muffin liners in the air fryer basket and bake for 14 minutes (or until the tops are browned and a toothpick inserted in the center comes out clean). Carefully remove the muffins from the basket and repeat with the remaining batter and topping.

9. Serve warm.

# Fried Pb&j

Servings: 4

Cooking Time: 8 Minutes

**Ingredients:**

- ½ cup cornflakes, crushed
- ¼ cup shredded coconut
- 8 slices oat nut bread or any whole-grain, oversize bread
- 6 tablespoons peanut butter
- 2 medium bananas, cut into ½-inch-thick slices
- 6 tablespoons pineapple preserves
- 1 egg, beaten
- oil for misting or cooking spray

**Directions:**

1. Preheat air fryer to 360°F.

2. In a shallow dish, mix together the cornflake crumbs and coconut.

3. For each sandwich, spread one bread slice with 1½ tablespoons of peanut butter. Top with banana slices. Spread another bread slice with 1½ tablespoons of preserves. Combine to make a sandwich.

4. Using a pastry brush, brush top of sandwich lightly with beaten egg. Sprinkle with about 1½ tablespoons of crumb coating, pressing it in to make it stick. Spray with oil.

5. Turn sandwich over and repeat to coat and spray the other side.

6. Cooking 2 at a time, place sandwiches in air fryer basket and cook for 6 to 7minutes or until coating is golden brown and crispy. If sandwich doesn't brown enough, spray with a little more oil and cook at 390°F for another minute.

7. Cut cooked sandwiches in half and serve warm.

# French Toast Sticks

Servings: 4

Cooking Time: 7 Minutes

**Ingredients:**

- 2 eggs
- ½ cup milk
- ⅛ teaspoon salt
- ½ teaspoon pure vanilla extract
- ¾ cup crushed cornflakes
- 6 slices sandwich bread, each slice cut into 4 strips
- oil for misting or cooking spray
- maple syrup or honey

**Directions:**

1. In a small bowl, beat together eggs, milk, salt, and vanilla.
2. Place crushed cornflakes on a plate or in a shallow dish.
3. Dip bread strips in egg mixture, shake off excess, and roll in cornflake crumbs.
4. Spray both sides of bread strips with oil.
5. Place bread strips in air fryer basket in single layer.
6. Cook at 390°F for 7minutes or until they're dark golden brown.
7. Repeat steps 5 and 6 to cook remaining French toast sticks.
8. Serve with maple syrup or honey for dipping.

# DESSERTS AND SWEETS

## Cherry Hand Pies

Servings: 8

Cooking Time: 8 Minutes

**Ingredients:**

- 4 cups frozen or canned pitted tart cherries (if using canned, drain and pat dry)
- 2 teaspoons lemon juice
- ½ cup sugar
- ¼ cup cornstarch
- 1 teaspoon vanilla extract
- 1 Basic Pie Dough (see the preceding recipe) or store-bought pie dough

**Directions:**

1. In a medium saucepan, place the cherries and lemon juice and cook over medium heat for 10 minutes, or until the cherries begin to break down.

2. In a small bowl, stir together the sugar and cornstarch. Pour the sugar mixture into the cherries, stirring constantly. Cook the cherry mixture over low heat for 2 to 3 minutes, or until thickened. Remove from the heat and stir in the vanilla extract. Allow the cherry mixture to cool to room temperature, about 30 minutes.

3. Meanwhile, bring the pie dough to room temperature. Divide the dough into 8 equal pieces. Roll out the dough to ¼-inch thickness in circles. Place ¼ cup filling in the center of each rolled dough. Fold the dough to create a half-circle. Using a fork, press around the edges to seal the hand pies. Pierce the top of the pie with a fork for steam release while cooking. Continue until 8 hand pies are formed.

4. Preheat the air fryer to 350°F.

5. Place a single layer of hand pies in the air fryer basket and spray with cooking spray. Cook for 8 to 10 minutes or until golden brown and cooked through.

# Coconut Crusted Bananas With Pineapple Sauce

Servings: 4

Cooking Time: 5 Minutes

**Ingredients:**

- Pineapple Sauce
- 1½ cups puréed fresh pineapple
- 2 tablespoons sugar
- juice of 1 lemon
- ¼ teaspoon ground cinnamon
- 3 firm bananas
- ¼ cup sweetened condensed milk
- 1¼ cups shredded coconut
- ⅓ cup crushed graham crackers (crumbs)*
- vegetable or canola oil, in a spray bottle
- vanilla frozen yogurt or ice cream

**Directions:**

1. Make the pineapple sauce by combining the pineapple, sugar, lemon juice and cinnamon in a saucepan. Simmer the mixture on the stovetop for 20 minutes, and then set it aside.

2. Slice the bananas diagonally into ½-inch thick slices and place them in a bowl. Pour the sweetened condensed milk into the bowl and toss the bananas gently to coat. Combine the coconut and graham cracker crumbs together in a shallow dish. Remove the banana slices from the condensed milk and let any excess milk drip off. Dip the banana slices in the coconut and crumb mixture to coat both sides. Spray the coated slices with oil.

3. Preheat the air fryer to 400°F.

4. Grease the bottom of the air fryer basket with a little oil. Air-fry the bananas in batches at 400°F for 5 minutes, turning them over halfway through the cooking time. Air-fry until the bananas are golden brown on both sides.

5. Serve warm over vanilla frozen yogurt with some of the pineapple sauce spooned over top.

# Fried Cannoli Wontons

Servings: 10

Cooking Time: 8 Minutes

**Ingredients:**

- 8 ounces Neufchâtel cream cheese
- ¼ cup powdered sugar
- 1 teaspoon vanilla extract
- ¼ teaspoon salt
- ¼ cup mini chocolate chips
- 2 tablespoons chopped pecans (optional)
- 20 wonton wrappers
- ¼ cup filtered water

**Directions:**

1. Preheat the air fryer to 370°F.
2. In a large bowl, use a hand mixer to combine the cream cheese with the powdered sugar, vanilla, and salt. Fold in the chocolate chips and pecans. Set aside.
3. Lay the wonton wrappers out on a flat, smooth surface and place a bowl with the filtered water next to them.
4. Use a teaspoon to evenly divide the cream cheese mixture among the 20 wonton wrappers, placing the batter in the center of the wontons.
5. Wet the tip of your index finger, and gently moisten the outer edges of the wrapper. Then fold each wrapper until it creates a secure pocket.
6. Liberally spray the air fryer basket with olive oil mist.
7. Place the wontons into the basket, and cook for 5 to 8 minutes. When the outer edges begin to brown, remove the wontons from the air fryer basket. Repeat cooking with remaining wontons.
8. Serve warm.

# Apple Crisp

Servings: 4

Cooking Time: 16 Minutes

**Ingredients:**

- Filling
- 3 Granny Smith apples, thinly sliced (about 4 cups)
- ¼ teaspoon ground cinnamon
- ⅛ teaspoon salt
- 1½ teaspoons lemon juice
- 2 tablespoons honey
- 1 tablespoon brown sugar
- cooking spray
- Crumb Topping
- 2 tablespoons oats
- 2 tablespoons oat bran
- 2 tablespoons cooked quinoa
- 2 tablespoons chopped walnuts
- 2 tablespoons brown sugar
- 2 teaspoons coconut oil

**Directions:**

1. Combine all filling ingredients and stir well so that apples are evenly coated.

2. Spray air fryer baking pan with nonstick cooking spray and spoon in the apple mixture.

3. Cook at 360°F for 5minutes. Stir well, scooping up from the bottom to mix apples and sauce.

4. At this point, the apples should be crisp-tender. Continue cooking in 3-minute intervals until apples are as soft as you like.

5. While apples are cooking, combine all topping ingredients in a small bowl. Stir until coconut oil mixes in well and distributes evenly. If your coconut oil is cold, it may be easier to mix in by hand.

6. When apples are cooked to your liking, sprinkle crumb mixture on top. Cook at 360°F for 8 minutes or until crumb topping is golden brown and crispy.

# Gingerbread

Servings: 6

Cooking Time: 20 Minutes

**Ingredients:**

- cooking spray
- 1 cup flour
- 2 tablespoons sugar
- ¾ teaspoon ground ginger
- ¼ teaspoon cinnamon
- 1 teaspoon baking powder
- ½ teaspoon baking soda
- ⅛ teaspoon salt
- 1 egg
- ¼ cup molasses
- ½ cup buttermilk
- 2 tablespoons oil
- 1 teaspoon pure vanilla extract

**Directions:**

1. Preheat air fryer to 330°F.
2. Spray 6 x 6-inch baking dish lightly with cooking spray.
3. In a medium bowl, mix together all the dry ingredients.
4. In a separate bowl, beat the egg. Add molasses, buttermilk, oil, and vanilla and stir until well mixed.
5. Pour liquid mixture into dry ingredients and stir until well blended.
6. Pour batter into baking dish and cook at 330°F for 20minutes or until toothpick inserted in center of loaf comes out clean.

# Strawberry Pastry Rolls

Servings: 4                                                    Cooking Time: 6 Minutes

## Ingredients:

- 3 ounces low-fat cream cheese
- 2 tablespoons plain yogurt
- 2 teaspoons sugar
- ¼ teaspoon pure vanilla extract
- 8 ounces fresh strawberries
- 8 sheets phyllo dough
- butter-flavored cooking spray
- ¼–½ cup dark chocolate chips (optional)

## Directions:

1.  In a medium bowl, combine the cream cheese, yogurt, sugar, and vanilla. Beat with hand mixer at high speed until smooth, about 1 minute.

2.  Wash strawberries and destem. Chop enough of them to measure ½ cup. Stir into cheese mixture.

3.  Preheat air fryer to 330°F.

4.  Phyllo dough dries out quickly, so cover your stack of phyllo sheets with waxed paper and then place a damp dish towel on top of that. Remove only one sheet at a time as you work.

5.  To create one pastry roll, lay out a single sheet of phyllo. Spray lightly with butter-flavored spray, top with a second sheet of phyllo, and spray the second sheet lightly.

6.  Place a quarter of the filling (about 3 tablespoons) about ½ inch from the edge of one short side. Fold the end of the phyllo over the filling and keep rolling a turn or two. Fold in both the left and right sides so that the edges meet in the middle of your roll. Then roll up completely. Spray outside of pastry roll with butter spray.

7.  When you have 4 rolls, place them in the air fryer basket, seam side down, leaving some space in between each. Cook at 330°F for 6 minutes, until they turn a delicate golden brown.

8.  Repeat step 7 for remaining rolls.

9.  Allow pastries to cool to room temperature.

10. When ready to serve, slice the remaining strawberries. If desired, melt the chocolate chips in microwave or double boiler. Place 1 pastry on each dessert plate, and top with sliced strawberries. Drizzle melted chocolate over strawberries and onto plate.

# Nutella® Torte

Servings: 6                                                Cooking Time: 55 Minutes

**Ingredients:**

- ¼ cup unsalted butter, softened
- ½ cup sugar
- 2 eggs
- 1 teaspoon vanilla
- 1¼ cups Nutella® (or other chocolate hazelnut spread), divided
- ¼ cup flour
- 1 teaspoon baking powder
- ¼ teaspoon salt
- dark chocolate fudge topping
- coarsely chopped toasted hazelnuts

**Directions:**

1. Cream the butter and sugar together with an electric hand mixer until light and fluffy. Add the eggs, vanilla, and ¾ cup of the Nutella® and mix until combined. Combine the flour, baking powder and salt together, and add these dry ingredients to the butter mixture, beating for 1 minute.

2. Preheat the air fryer to 350°F.

3. Grease a 7-inch cake pan with butter and then line the bottom of the pan with a circle of parchment paper. Grease the parchment paper circle as well. Pour the batter into the prepared cake pan and wrap the pan completely with aluminum foil. Lower the pan into the air fryer basket with an aluminum sling (fold a piece of aluminum foil into a strip about 2-inches wide by 24-inches long). Fold the ends of the aluminum foil over the top of the dish before returning the basket to the air fryer. Air-fry for 30 minutes. Remove the foil and air-fry for another 25 minutes.

4. Remove the cake from air fryer and let it cool for 10 minutes. Invert the cake onto a plate, remove the parchment paper and invert the cake back onto a serving platter. While the cake is still warm, spread the remaining ½ cup of Nutella® over the top of the cake. Melt the dark chocolate fudge in the microwave for about 10 seconds so it melts enough to be pourable. Drizzle the sauce on top of the cake in a zigzag motion. Turn the cake 90 degrees and drizzle more sauce in zigzags perpendicular to the first zigzags. Garnish the edges of the torte with the toasted hazelnuts and serve.

# Fried Twinkies

Servings:6

Cooking Time: 5 Minutes

**Ingredients:**

- ➢ 2 Large egg white(s)
- ➢ 2 tablespoons Water
- ➢ 1½ cups (about 9 ounces) Ground gingersnap cookie crumbs
- ➢ 6 Twinkies
- ➢ Vegetable oil spray

**Directions:**

1. Preheat the air fryer to 400°F.

2. Set up and fill two shallow soup plates or small pie plates on your counter: one for the egg white(s), whisked with the water until foamy; and one for the gingersnap crumbs.

3. Dip a Twinkie in the egg white(s), turning it to coat on all sides, even the ends. Let the excess egg white mixture slip back into the rest, then set the Twinkie in the crumbs. Roll it to coat on all sides, even the ends, pressing gently to get an even coating. Then repeat this process: egg white(s), followed by crumbs. Lightly coat the prepared Twinkie on all sides with vegetable oil spray. Set aside and coat each of the remaining Twinkies with the same double-dipping technique, followed by spraying.

4. Set the Twinkies flat side up in the basket with as much air space between them as possible. Air-fry for 5 minutes, or until browned and crunchy.

5. Use a nonstick-safe spatula to gently transfer the Twinkies to a wire rack. Cool for at least 10 minutes before serving.

# Oreo-coated Peanut Butter Cups

Servings:8

Cooking Time: 4 Minutes

**Ingredients:**

- 8 Standard ¾-ounce peanut butter cups, frozen
- ⅓ cup All-purpose flour
- 2 Large egg white(s), beaten until foamy
- 16 Oreos or other creme-filled chocolate sandwich cookies, ground to crumbs in a food processor
- Vegetable oil spray

**Directions:**

1. Set up and fill three shallow soup plates or small pie plates on your counter: one for the flour, one for the beaten egg white(s), and one for the cookie crumbs.

2. Dip a frozen peanut butter cup in the flour, turning it to coat all sides. Shake off any excess, then set it in the beaten egg white(s). Turn it to coat all sides, then let any excess egg white slip back into the rest. Set the candy bar in the cookie crumbs. Turn to coat on all parts, even the sides. Dip the peanut butter cup back in the egg white(s) as before, then into the cookie crumbs as before, making sure you have a solid, even coating all around the cup. Set aside while you dip and coat the remaining cups.

3. When all the peanut butter cups are dipped and coated, lightly coat them on all sides with the vegetable oil spray. Set them on a plate and freeze while the air fryer heats.

4. Preheat the air fryer to 400°F.

5. Set the dipped cups wider side up in the basket with as much air space between them as possible. Air-fry undisturbed for 4 minutes, or until they feel soft but the coating is set.

6. Turn off the machine and remove the basket from it. Set aside the basket with the fried cups for 10 minutes. Use a nonstick-safe spatula to transfer the fried cups to a wire rack. Cool for at least another 5 minutes before serving.

# Baked Apple

Servings: 6

Cooking Time: 20 Minutes

**Ingredients:**

- ➢ 3 small Honey Crisp or other baking apples
- ➢ 3 tablespoons maple syrup
- ➢ 3 tablespoons chopped pecans
- ➢ 1 tablespoon firm butter, cut into 6 pieces

**Directions:**

1. Put ½ cup water in the drawer of the air fryer.
2. Wash apples well and dry them.
3. Split apples in half. Remove core and a little of the flesh to make a cavity for the pecans.
4. Place apple halves in air fryer basket, cut side up.
5. Spoon 1½ teaspoons pecans into each cavity.
6. Spoon ½ tablespoon maple syrup over pecans in each apple.
7. Top each apple with ½ teaspoon butter.
8. Cook at 360°F for 20 minutes, until apples are tender.

# Chewy Coconut Cake

Servings: 6
Cooking Time: 18-22 Minutes

**Ingredients:**

- ¾ cup plus 2½ tablespoons All-purpose flour
- ¾ teaspoon Baking powder
- ⅛ teaspoon Table salt
- 7½ tablespoons (1 stick minus ½ tablespoon) Butter, at room temperature
- ⅓ cup plus 1 tablespoon Granulated white sugar
- 5 tablespoons Packed light brown sugar
- 5 tablespoons Pasteurized egg substitute, such as Egg Beaters
- 2 teaspoons Vanilla extract
- ½ cup Unsweetened shredded coconut (see here)
- Baking spray

**Directions:**

1. Preheat the air fryer to 325°F (or 330°F, if that's the closest setting).

2. Mix the flour, baking powder, and salt in a small bowl until well combined.

3. Using an electric hand mixer at medium speed , beat the butter, granulated white sugar, and brown sugar in a medium bowl until creamy and smooth, about 3 minutes, occasionally scraping down the inside of the bowl. Beat in the egg substitute or egg and vanilla until smooth.

4. Scrape down and remove the beaters. Fold in the flour mixture with a rubber spatula just until all the flour is moistened. Fold in the coconut until the mixture is a uniform color.

5. Use the baking spray to generously coat the inside of a 6-inch round cake pan for a small batch, a 7-inch round cake pan for a medium batch, or an 8-inch round cake pan for a large batch. Scrape and spread the batter into the pan, smoothing the batter out to an even layer.

6. Set the pan in the basket and air-fry for 18 minutes for a 6-inch layer, 20 minutes for a 7-inch layer, or 22 minutes for an 8-inch layer, or until the cake is well browned and set even if there's a little soft give right at the center. Start checking it at the 16-minute mark to know where you are.

7. Use hot pads or silicone baking mitts to transfer the cake pan to a wire rack. Cool for at least 1 hour or up to 4 hours. Use a nonstick-safe knife to slice the cake into wedges right in the pan, lifting them out one by one.

# Chocolate Macaroons

Servings: 16

Cooking Time: 8 Minutes

**Ingredients:**

- ➢ 2 Large egg white(s), at room temperature
- ➢ ⅛ teaspoon Table salt
- ➢ ½ cup Granulated white sugar
- ➢ 1½ cups Unsweetened shredded coconut
- ➢ 3 tablespoons Unsweetened cocoa powder

**Directions:**

1. Preheat the air fryer to 375°F .

2. Using an electric mixer at high speed, beat the egg white(s) and salt in a medium or large bowl until stiff peaks can be formed when the turned-off beaters are dipped into the mixture.

3. Still working with the mixer at high speed, beat in the sugar in a slow stream until the meringue is shiny and thick.

4. Scrape down and remove the beaters. Fold in the coconut and cocoa with a rubber spatula until well combined, working carefully to deflate the meringue as little as possible.

5. Scoop up 2 tablespoons of the mixture. Wet your clean hands and roll that little bit of coconut bliss into a ball. Set it aside and continue making more balls: 7 more for a small batch, 15 more for a medium batch, or 23 more for a large one.

6. Line the bottom of the machine's basket or the basket attachment with parchment paper. Set the balls on the parchment with as much air space between them as possible. Air-fry undisturbed for 8 minutes, or until dry, set, and lightly browned.

7. Use a nonstick-safe spatula to transfer the macaroons to a wire rack. Cool for at least 10 minutes before serving. Or cool to room temperature, about 30 minutes, then store in a sealed container at room temperature for up to 3 days.

# VEGETARIANS RECIPES

## Charred Cauliflower Tacos

Servings: 4                                                       Cooking Time: 10 Minutes

**Ingredients:**

- 1 head cauliflower, washed and cut into florets
- 2 tablespoons avocado oil
- 2 teaspoons taco seasoning
- 1 medium avocado
- ½ teaspoon garlic powder
- ¼ teaspoon black pepper
- ¼ teaspoon salt
- 2 tablespoons chopped red onion
- 2 teaspoons fresh squeezed lime juice
- ¼ cup chopped cilantro
- Eight 6-inch corn tortillas
- ½ cup cooked corn
- ½ cup shredded purple cabbage

**Directions:**

1. Preheat the air fryer to 390°F.

2. In a large bowl, toss the cauliflower with the avocado oil and taco seasoning. Set the metal trivet inside the air fryer basket and liberally spray with olive oil.

3. Place the cauliflower onto the trivet and cook for 10 minutes, shaking every 3 minutes to allow for an even char.

4. While the cauliflower is cooking, prepare the avocado sauce. In a medium bowl, mash the avocado; then mix in the garlic powder, pepper, salt, and onion. Stir in the lime juice and cilantro; set aside.

5. Remove the cauliflower from the air fryer basket.

6. Place 1 tablespoon of avocado sauce in the middle of a tortilla, and top with corn, cabbage, and charred cauliflower. Repeat with the remaining tortillas. Serve immediately.

# Spinach And Cheese Calzone

Servings: 2

Cooking Time: 10 Minutes

**Ingredients:**

➢ ⅔ cup frozen chopped spinach, thawed

➢ 1 cup grated mozzarella cheese

➢ 1 cup ricotta cheese

➢ ½ teaspoon Italian seasoning

➢ ½ teaspoon salt

➢ freshly ground black pepper

➢ 1 store-bought or homemade pizza dough* (about 12 to 16 ounces)

➢ 2 tablespoons olive oil

➢ pizza or marinara sauce (optional)

**Directions:**

1.  Drain and squeeze all the water out of the thawed spinach and set it aside. Mix the mozzarella cheese, ricotta cheese, Italian seasoning, salt and freshly ground black pepper together in a bowl. Stir in the chopped spinach.

2.  Divide the dough in half. With floured hands or on a floured surface, stretch or roll one half of the dough into a 10-inch circle. Spread half of the cheese and spinach mixture on half of the dough, leaving about one inch of dough empty around the edge.

3.  Fold the other half of the dough over the cheese mixture, almost to the edge of the bottom dough to form a half moon. Fold the bottom edge of dough up over the top edge and crimp the dough around the edges in order to make the crust and seal the calzone. Brush the dough with olive oil. Repeat with the second half of dough to make the second calzone.

4.  Preheat the air fryer to 360°F.

5.  Brush or spray the air fryer basket with olive oil. Air-fry the calzones one at a time for 10 minutes, flipping the calzone over half way through. Serve with warm pizza or marinara sauce if desired.

# Eggplant Parmesan

Servings: 4

Cooking Time: 8 Minutes Per Batch

**Ingredients:**

- ➢ 1 medium eggplant, 6–8 inches long
- ➢ salt
- ➢ 1 large egg
- ➢ 1 tablespoon water
- ➢ ⅔ cup panko breadcrumbs
- ➢ ⅓ cup grated Parmesan cheese, plus more for serving
- ➢ 1 tablespoon Italian seasoning
- ➢ ¾ teaspoon oregano
- ➢ oil for misting or cooking spray
- ➢ 1 24-ounce jar marinara sauce
- ➢ 8 ounces spaghetti, cooked
- ➢ pepper

**Directions:**

1. Preheat air fryer to 390°F.
2. Leaving peel intact, cut eggplant into 8 round slices about ¾-inch thick. Salt to taste.
3. Beat egg and water in a shallow dish.
4. In another shallow dish, combine panko, Parmesan, Italian seasoning, and oregano.
5. Dip eggplant slices in egg wash and then crumbs, pressing lightly to coat.
6. Mist slices with oil or cooking spray.
7. Place 4 eggplant slices in air fryer basket and cook for 8 minutes, until brown and crispy.
8. While eggplant is cooking, heat marinara sauce.
9. Repeat step 7 to cook remaining eggplant slices.
10. To serve, place cooked spaghetti on plates and top with marinara and eggplant slices. At the table, pass extra Parmesan cheese and freshly ground black pepper.

# Mushroom, Zucchini And Black Bean Burgers

Servings: 4      Cooking Time: 18 Minutes

**Ingredients:**

- 1 cup diced zucchini, (about ½ medium zucchini)
- 1 tablespoon olive oil
- salt and freshly ground black pepper
- 1 cup chopped brown mushrooms (about 3 ounces)
- 1 small clove garlic
- 1 (15-ounce) can black beans, drained and rinsed
- 1 teaspoon lemon zest
- 1 tablespoon chopped fresh cilantro
- ½ cup plain breadcrumbs
- 1 egg, beaten
- ½ teaspoon salt
- freshly ground black pepper
- whole-wheat pita bread, burger buns or brioche buns
- mayonnaise, tomato, avocado and lettuce, for serving

**Directions:**

1. Preheat the air fryer to 400°F.

2. Toss the zucchini with the olive oil, season with salt and freshly ground black pepper and air-fry for 6 minutes, shaking the basket once or twice while it cooks.

3. Transfer the zucchini to a food processor with the mushrooms, garlic and black beans and process until still a little chunky but broken down and pasty. Transfer the mixture to a bowl. Add the lemon zest, cilantro, breadcrumbs and egg and mix well. Season again with salt and freshly ground black pepper. Shape the mixture into four burger patties and refrigerate for at least 15 minutes.

4. Preheat the air fryer to 370°F. Transfer two of the veggie burgers to the air fryer basket and air-fry for 12 minutes, flipping the burgers gently halfway through the cooking time. Keep the burgers warm by loosely tenting them with foil while you cook the remaining two burgers. Return the first batch of burgers back into the air fryer with the second batch for the last two minutes of cooking to re-heat.

5. Serve on toasted whole-wheat pita bread, burger buns or brioche buns with some mayonnaise, tomato, avocado and lettuce.

# Black Bean Empanadas

Servings: 12

Cooking Time: 35 Minutes

**Ingredients:**

- 1½ cups all-purpose flour
- 1 cup whole-wheat flour
- 1 teaspoon salt
- ½ cup cold unsalted butter
- 1 egg
- ½ cup milk
- One 14.5-ounce can black beans, drained and rinsed
- ¼ cup chopped cilantro
- 1 cup shredded purple cabbage
- 1 cup shredded Monterey jack cheese
- ¼ cup salsa

**Directions:**

1.  In a food processor, place the all-purpose flour, whole-wheat flour, salt, and butter into processor and process for 2 minutes, scraping down the sides of the food processor every 30 seconds. Add in the egg and blend for 30 seconds. Using the pulse button, add in the milk 1 tablespoon at a time, or until dough is moist enough to handle and be rolled into a ball. Let the dough rest at room temperature for 30 minutes.

2.  Meanwhile, in a large bowl, mix together the black beans, cilantro, cabbage, Monterey Jack cheese, and salsa.

3.  On a floured surface, cut the dough in half; then form a ball and cut each ball into 6 equal pieces, totaling 12 equal pieces. Work with one piece at a time, and cover the remaining dough with a towel.

4.  Roll out a piece of dough into a 6-inch round, much like a tortilla, ¼ inch thick. Place 4 tablespoons of filling in the center of the round, and fold over to form a half-circle. Using a fork, crimp the edges together and pierce the top for air holes. Repeat with the remaining dough and filling.

5.  Preheat the air fryer to 350°F.

6.  Working in batches, place 3 to 4 empanadas in the air fryer basket and spray with cooking spray. Cook for 4 minutes, flip over the empanadas and spray with cooking spray, and cook another 4 minutes.

# Cheesy Enchilada Stuffed Baked Potatoes

Servings: 4                                      Cooking Time: 37 Minutes

**Ingredients:**

- 2 medium russet potatoes, washed
- One 15-ounce can mild red enchilada sauce
- One 15-ounce can low-sodium black beans, rinsed and drained
- 1 teaspoon taco seasoning
- ½ cup shredded cheddar cheese
- 1 medium avocado, halved
- ½ teaspoon garlic powder
- ¼ teaspoon black pepper
- ¼ teaspoon salt
- 2 teaspoons fresh lime juice
- 2 tablespoon chopped red onion
- ¼ cup chopped cilantro

**Directions:**

1. Preheat the air fryer to 390°F.
2. Puncture the outer surface of the potatoes with a fork.
3. Set the potatoes inside the air fryer basket and cook for 20 minutes, rotate, and cook another 10 minutes.
4. In a large bowl, mix the enchilada sauce, black beans, and taco seasoning.
5. When the potatoes have finished cooking, carefully remove them from the air fryer basket and let cool for 5 minutes.
6. Using a pair of tongs to hold the potato if it's still too hot to touch, slice the potato in half lengthwise. Use a spoon to scoop out the potato flesh and add it into the bowl with the enchilada sauce. Mash the potatoes with the enchilada sauce mixture, creating a uniform stuffing.
7. Place the potato skins into an air-fryer-safe pan and stuff the halves with the enchilada stuffing. Sprinkle the cheese over the top of each potato.
8. Set the air fryer temperature to 350°F, return the pan to the air fryer basket, and cook for another 5 to 7 minutes to heat the potatoes and melt the cheese.
9. While the potatoes are cooking, take the avocado and scoop out the flesh into a small bowl. Mash it with the back of a fork; then mix in the garlic powder, pepper, salt, lime juice, and onion. Set aside.
10. When the potatoes have finished cooking, remove the pan from the air fryer and place the potato halves on a plate. Top with avocado mash and fresh cilantro. Serve immediately.

# Roasted Vegetable Thai Green Curry

Servings: 4

Cooking Time: 16 Minutes

**Ingredients:**

- 1 (13-ounce) can coconut milk
- 3 tablespoons green curry paste
- 1 tablespoon soy sauce*
- 1 tablespoon rice wine vinegar
- 1 teaspoon sugar
- 1 teaspoon minced fresh ginger
- ½ onion, chopped
- 3 carrots, sliced
- 1 red bell pepper, chopped
- olive oil
- 10 stalks of asparagus, cut into 2-inch pieces
- 3 cups broccoli florets
- basmati rice for serving
- fresh cilantro
- crushed red pepper flakes (optional)

**Directions:**

1. Combine the coconut milk, green curry paste, soy sauce, rice wine vinegar, sugar and ginger in a medium saucepan and bring to a boil on the stovetop. Reduce the heat and simmer for 20 minutes while you cook the vegetables. Set aside.

2. Preheat the air fryer to 400°F.

3. Toss the onion, carrots, and red pepper together with a little olive oil and transfer the vegetables to the air fryer basket. Air-fry at 400°F for 10 minutes, shaking the basket a few times during the cooking process. Add the asparagus and broccoli florets and air-fry for an additional 6 minutes, again shaking the basket for even cooking.

4. When the vegetables are cooked to your liking, toss them with the green curry sauce and serve in bowls over basmati rice. Garnish with fresh chopped cilantro and crushed red pepper flakes.

# Asparagus, Mushroom And Cheese Soufflés

Servings: 3                                          Cooking Time: 21 Minutes

**Ingredients:**

- butter
- grated Parmesan cheese
- 3 button mushrooms, thinly sliced
- 8 spears asparagus, sliced ½-inch long
- 1 teaspoon olive oil
- 1 tablespoon butter
- 4½ teaspoons flour
- pinch paprika
- pinch ground nutmeg
- salt and freshly ground black pepper
- ½ cup milk
- ½ cup grated Gruyère cheese or other Swiss cheese (about 2 ounces)
- 2 eggs, separated

**Directions:**

1. Butter three 6-ounce ramekins and dust with grated Parmesan cheese. (Butter the ramekins and then coat the butter with Parmesan by shaking it around in the ramekin and dumping out any excess.)

2. Preheat the air fryer to 400°F.

3. Toss the mushrooms and asparagus in a bowl with the olive oil. Transfer the vegetables to the air fryer and air-fry for 7 minutes, shaking the basket once or twice to redistribute the Ingredients while they cook.

4. While the vegetables are cooking, make the soufflé base. Melt the butter in a saucepan on the stovetop over medium heat. Add the flour, stir and cook for a minute or two. Add the paprika, nutmeg, salt and pepper. Whisk in the milk and bring the mixture to a simmer to thicken. Remove the pan from the heat and add the cheese, stirring to melt. Let the mixture cool for just a few minutes and then whisk the egg yolks in, one at a time. Stir in the cooked mushrooms and asparagus. Let this soufflé base cool.

5. In a separate bowl, whisk the egg whites to soft peak stage (the point at which the whites can almost stand up on the end of your whisk). Fold the whipped egg whites into the soufflé base, adding a little at a time.

6. Preheat the air fryer to 330°F.

7. Transfer the batter carefully to the buttered ramekins, leaving about ½-inch at the top. Place the ramekins into the air fryer basket and air-fry for 14 minutes. The soufflés should have risen nicely and be brown on top. Serve immediately.

# Quinoa Burgers With Feta Cheese And Dill

Servings: 6                                        Cooking Time: 10 Minutes

**Ingredients:**

- 1 cup quinoa (red, white or multi-colored)
- 1½ cups water
- 1 teaspoon salt
- freshly ground black pepper
- 1½ cups rolled oats
- 3 eggs, lightly beaten
- ¼ cup minced white onion
- ½ cup crumbled feta cheese
- ¼ cup chopped fresh dill
- salt and freshly ground black pepper
- vegetable or canola oil, in a spray bottle
- whole-wheat hamburger buns (or gluten-free hamburger buns*)
- arugula
- tomato, sliced
- red onion, sliced
- mayonnaise

**Directions:**

1. Make the quinoa: Rinse the quinoa in cold water in a saucepan, swirling it with your hand until any dry husks rise to the surface. Drain the quinoa as well as you can and then put the saucepan on the stovetop to dry and toast the quinoa. Turn the heat to medium-high and shake the pan regularly until you see the quinoa moving easily and can hear the seeds moving in the pan, indicating that they are dry. Add the water, salt and pepper. Bring the liquid to a boil and then reduce the heat to low or medium-low. You should see just a few bubbles, not a boil. Cover with a lid, leaving it askew and simmer for 20 minutes. Turn the heat off and fluff the quinoa with a fork. If there's any liquid left in the bottom of the pot, place it back on the burner for another 3 minutes or so. Spread the cooked quinoa out on a sheet pan to cool.

2. Combine the room temperature quinoa in a large bowl with the oats, eggs, onion, cheese and dill. Season with salt and pepper and mix well (remember that feta cheese is salty). Shape the mixture into 6 patties with flat sides (so they fit more easily into the air fryer). Add a little water or a few more rolled oats if necessary to get the mixture to be the right consistency to make patties.

3. Preheat the air-fryer to 400°F.

4. Spray both sides of the patties generously with oil and transfer them to the air fryer basket in one layer (you will probably have to cook these burgers in batches, depending on the size of your air fryer). Air-fry each batch at 400°F for 10 minutes, flipping the burgers over halfway through the cooking time.

5. Build your burger on the whole-wheat hamburger buns with arugula, tomato, red onion and mayonnaise.

# Egg Rolls

Servings: 4

Cooking Time: 8 Minutes

**Ingredients:**

- 1 clove garlic, minced
- 1 teaspoon sesame oil
- 1 teaspoon olive oil
- ½ cup chopped celery
- ½ cup grated carrots
- 2 green onions, chopped
- 2 ounces mushrooms, chopped
- 2 cups shredded Napa cabbage
- 1 teaspoon low-sodium soy sauce
- 1 teaspoon cornstarch
- salt
- 1 egg
- 1 tablespoon water
- 4 egg roll wraps
- olive oil for misting or cooking spray

**Directions:**

1. In a large skillet, sauté garlic in sesame and olive oils over medium heat for 1 minute.
2. Add celery, carrots, onions, and mushrooms to skillet. Cook 1 minute, stirring.
3. Stir in cabbage, cover, and cook for 1 minute or just until cabbage slightly wilts.
4. In a small bowl, mix soy sauce and cornstarch. Stir into vegetables to thicken. Remove from heat. Salt to taste if needed.
5. Beat together egg and water in a small bowl.
6. Divide filling into 4 portions and roll up in egg roll wraps. Brush all over with egg wash to seal.
7. Mist egg rolls very lightly with olive oil or cooking spray and place in air fryer basket.
8. Cook at 390°F for 4minutes. Turn over and cook 4 more minutes, until golden brown and crispy.

# Mexican Twice Air-fried Sweet Potatoes

Servings: 2

Cooking Time: 42 Minutes

**Ingredients:**

- 2 large sweet potatoes
- olive oil
- salt and freshly ground black pepper
- ⅓ cup diced red onion
- ⅓ cup diced red bell pepper
- ½ cup canned black beans, drained and rinsed
- ½ cup corn kernels, fresh or frozen
- ½ teaspoon chili powder
- 1½ cups grated pepper jack cheese, divided
- Jalapeño peppers, sliced

**Directions:**

1. Preheat the air fryer to 400°F.

2. Rub the outside of the sweet potatoes with olive oil and season with salt and freshly ground black pepper. Transfer the potatoes into the air fryer basket and air-fry at 400°F for 30 minutes, rotating the potatoes a few times during the cooking process.

3. While the potatoes are air-frying, start the potato filling. Preheat a large sauté pan over medium heat on the stovetop. Add the onion and pepper and sauté for a few minutes, until the vegetables start to soften. Add the black beans, corn, and chili powder and sauté for another 3 minutes. Set the mixture aside.

4. Remove the sweet potatoes from the air fryer and let them rest for 5 minutes. Slice off one inch of the flattest side of both potatoes. Scrape the potato flesh out of the potatoes, leaving half an inch of potato flesh around the edge of the potato. Place all the potato flesh into a large bowl and mash it with a fork. Add the black bean mixture and 1 cup of the pepper jack cheese to the mashed sweet potatoes. Season with salt and freshly ground black pepper and mix well. Stuff the hollowed out potato shells with the black bean and sweet potato mixture, mounding the filling high in the potatoes.

5. Transfer the stuffed potatoes back into the air fryer basket and air-fry at 370°F for 10 minutes. Sprinkle the remaining cheese on top of each stuffed potato, lower the heat to 340°F and air-fry for an additional 2 minutes to melt the cheese. Top with a couple slices of Jalapeño pepper and serve warm with a green salad.

# Spaghetti Squash And Kale Fritters With Pomodoro Sauce

Servings: 3                                    Cooking Time: 45 Minutes

**Ingredients:**

- 1½-pound spaghetti squash (about half a large or a whole small squash)
- olive oil
- ½ onion, diced
- ½ red bell pepper, diced
- 2 cloves garlic, minced
- 4 cups coarsely chopped kale
- salt and freshly ground black pepper
- 1 egg
- ⅓ cup breadcrumbs, divided*
- ⅓ cup grated Parmesan cheese
- ½ teaspoon dried rubbed sage
- pinch nutmeg
- Pomodoro Sauce:
- 2 tablespoons olive oil
- ½ onion, chopped
- 1 to 2 cloves garlic, minced
- 1 (28-ounce) can peeled tomatoes
- ¼ cup red wine
- 1 teaspoon Italian seasoning
- 2 tablespoons chopped fresh basil, plus more for garnish
- salt and freshly ground black pepper
- ½ teaspoon sugar (optional)

**Directions:**

1. Preheat the air fryer to 370°F.

2. Cut the spaghetti squash in half lengthwise and remove the seeds. Rub the inside of the squash with olive oil and season with salt and pepper. Place the squash, cut side up, into the air fryer basket and air-fry for 30 minutes, flipping the squash over halfway through the cooking process.

3. While the squash is cooking, Preheat a large sauté pan over medium heat on the stovetop. Add a little olive oil and sauté the onions for 3 minutes, until they start to soften. Add the red pepper and garlic and continue to sauté for an additional 4 minutes. Add the kale and season with salt and pepper. Cook for 2 more minutes, or until the kale is soft. Transfer the mixture to a large bowl and let it cool.

4. While the squash continues to cook, make the Pomodoro sauce. Preheat the large sauté pan again over medium heat on the stovetop. Add the olive oil and sauté the onion and garlic for 2 to 3 minutes, until the onion begins to soften. Crush the canned tomatoes with your hands and add them to the pan along with the red wine and Italian seasoning and simmer for 20 minutes. Add the basil and season to taste with salt, pepper and sugar (if using).

5. When the spaghetti squash has finished cooking, use a fork to scrape the inside flesh of the squash onto a sheet pan. Spread the squash out and let it cool.

6. Once cool, add the spaghetti squash to the kale mixture, along with the egg, breadcrumbs, Parmesan cheese, sage, nutmeg, salt and freshly ground black pepper. Stir to combine well and then divide the

mixture into 6 thick portions. You can shape the portions into patties, but I prefer to keep them a little random and unique in shape. Spray or brush the fritters with olive oil.

7.  Preheat the air fryer to 370°F.

8.  Brush the air fryer basket with a little olive oil and transfer the fritters to the basket. Air-fry the squash and kale fritters at 370°F for 15 minutes, flipping them over halfway through the cooking process.

9.  Serve the fritters warm with the Pomodoro sauce spooned over the top or pooled on your plate. Garnish with the fresh basil leaves.

# FISH AND SEAFOOD RECIPES

## Beer-battered Cod

Servings:3

Cooking Time: 12 Minutes

**Ingredients:**

- ➢ 1½ cups All-purpose flour
- ➢ 3 tablespoons Old Bay seasoning
- ➢ 1 Large egg(s)
- ➢ ¼ cup Amber beer, pale ale, or IPA
- ➢ 3 4-ounce skinless cod fillets
- ➢ Vegetable oil spray

**Directions:**

1. Preheat the air fryer to 400°F.

2. Set up and fill two shallow soup plates or small pie plates on your counter: one with the flour, whisked with the Old Bay until well combined; and one with the egg(s), whisked with the beer until foamy and uniform.

3. Dip a piece of cod in the flour mixture, turning it to coat on all sides (not just the top and bottom). Gently shake off any excess flour and dip the fish in the egg mixture, turning it to coat. Let any excess egg mixture slip back into the rest, then set the fish back in the flour mixture and coat it again, then back in the egg mixture for a second wash, then back in the flour mixture for a third time. Coat the fish on all sides with vegetable oil spray and set it aside. "Batter" the remaining piece(s) of cod in the same way.

4. Set the coated cod fillets in the basket with as much space between them as possible. They should not touch. Air-fry undisturbed for 12 minutes, or until brown and crisp.

5. Use kitchen tongs to gently transfer the fish to a wire rack. Cool for only a couple of minutes before serving.

# Black Cod With Grapes, Fennel, Pecans And Kale

Servings: 2

Cooking Time: 15 Minutes

**Ingredients:**

➢ 2 (6- to 8-ounce) fillets of black cod (or sablefish)

➢ salt and freshly ground black pepper

➢ olive oil

➢ 1 cup grapes, halved

➢ 1 small bulb fennel, sliced ¼-inch thick

➢ ½ cup pecans

➢ 3 cups shredded kale

➢ 2 teaspoons white balsamic vinegar or white wine vinegar

➢ 2 tablespoons extra virgin olive oil

**Directions:**

1.  Preheat the air fryer to 400°F.

2.  Season the cod fillets with salt and pepper and drizzle, brush or spray a little olive oil on top. Place the fish, presentation side up (skin side down), into the air fryer basket. Air-fry for 10 minutes.

3.  When the fish has finished cooking, remove the fillets to a side plate and loosely tent with foil to rest.

4.  Toss the grapes, fennel and pecans in a bowl with a drizzle of olive oil and season with salt and pepper. Add the grapes, fennel and pecans to the air fryer basket and air-fry for 5 minutes at 400°F, shaking the basket once during the cooking time.

5.  Transfer the grapes, fennel and pecans to a bowl with the kale. Dress the kale with the balsamic vinegar and olive oil, season to taste with salt and pepper and serve along side the cooked fish.

# Fried Oysters

Servings:12

Cooking Time: 8 Minutes

## Ingredients:

- 1½ cups All-purpose flour
- 1½ cups Yellow cornmeal
- 1½ tablespoons Cajun dried seasoning blend (for a homemade blend, see here)
- 1¼ cups, plus more if needed Amber beer, pale ale, or IPA
- 12 Large shucked oysters, any liquid drained off
- Vegetable oil spray

## Directions:

1. Preheat the air fryer to 400°F.

2. Whisk ⅔ cup of the flour, ½ cup of the cornmeal, and the seasoning blend in a bowl until uniform. Set aside.

3. Whisk the remaining ⅓ cup flour and the remaining ½ cup cornmeal with the beer in a second bowl, adding more beer in dribs and drabs until the mixture is the consistency of pancake batter.

4. Using a fork, dip a shucked oyster in the beer batter, coating it thoroughly. Gently shake off any excess batter, then set the oyster in the dry mixture and turn gently to coat well and evenly. Set the coated oyster on a cutting board and continue dipping and coating the remainder of the oysters.

5. Coat the oysters with vegetable oil spray, then set them in the basket with as much air space between them as possible. Air-fry undisturbed for 8 minutes, or until lightly browned and crisp.

6. Use a nonstick-safe spatula to transfer the oysters to a wire rack. Cool for a couple of minutes before serving.

# Crunchy Clam Strips

Servings:3

Cooking Time: 8 Minutes

**Ingredients:**

- ½ pound Clam strips, drained
- 1 Large egg, well beaten
- ½ cup All-purpose flour
- ½ cup Yellow cornmeal
- 1½ teaspoons Table salt
- 1½ teaspoons Ground black pepper
- Up to ¾ teaspoon Cayenne
- Vegetable oil spray

**Directions:**

1. Preheat the air fryer to 400°F.

2. Toss the clam strips and beaten egg in a bowl until the clams are well coated.

3. Mix the flour, cornmeal, salt, pepper, and cayenne in a large zip-closed plastic bag until well combined. Using a flatware fork or small kitchen tongs, lift the clam strips one by one out of the egg, letting any excess egg slip back into the rest. Put the strips in the bag with the flour mixture. Once all the strips are in the bag, seal it and shake gently until the strips are well coated.

4. Use kitchen tongs to pick out the clam strips and lay them on a cutting board (leaving any extra flour mixture in the bag to be discarded). Coat the strips on both sides with vegetable oil spray.

5. When the machine is at temperature, spread the clam strips in the basket in one layer. They may touch in places, but try to leave as much air space as possible around them. Air-fry undisturbed for 8 minutes, or until brown and crunchy.

6. Gently dump the contents of the basket onto a serving platter. Cool for just a minute or two before serving hot.

# Maple Balsamic Glazed Salmon

Servings: 4

Cooking Time: 10 Minutes

**Ingredients:**

- 4 (6-ounce) fillets of salmon
- salt and freshly ground black pepper
- vegetable oil
- ¼ cup pure maple syrup
- 3 tablespoons balsamic vinegar
- 1 teaspoon Dijon mustard

**Directions:**

1.  Preheat the air fryer to 400°F.

2.  Season the salmon well with salt and freshly ground black pepper. Spray or brush the bottom of the air fryer basket with vegetable oil and place the salmon fillets inside. Air-fry the salmon for 5 minutes.

3.  While the salmon is air-frying, combine the maple syrup, balsamic vinegar and Dijon mustard in a small saucepan over medium heat and stir to blend well. Let the mixture simmer while the fish is cooking. It should start to thicken slightly, but keep your eye on it so it doesn't burn.

4.  Brush the glaze on the salmon fillets and air-fry for an additional 5 minutes. The salmon should feel firm to the touch when finished and the glaze should be nicely browned on top. Brush a little more glaze on top before removing and serving with rice and vegetables, or a nice green salad.

# Pecan-crusted Tilapia

Servings: 4

Cooking Time: 8 Minutes

**Ingredients:**

- ➢ 1 pound skinless, boneless tilapia filets
- ➢ ¼ cup butter, melted
- ➢ 1 teaspoon minced fresh or dried rosemary
- ➢ 1 cup finely chopped pecans
- ➢ 1 teaspoon sea salt
- ➢ ¼ teaspoon paprika
- ➢ 2 tablespoons chopped parsley
- ➢ 1 lemon, cut into wedges

**Directions:**

1. Pat the tilapia filets dry with paper towels.
2. Pour the melted butter over the filets and flip the filets to coat them completely.
3. In a medium bowl, mix together the rosemary, pecans, salt, and paprika.
4. Preheat the air fryer to 350°F.
5. Place the tilapia filets into the air fryer basket and top with the pecan coating. Cook for 6 to 8 minutes. The fish should be firm to the touch and flake easily when fully cooked.
6. Remove the fish from the air fryer. Top the fish with chopped parsley and serve with lemon wedges.

# Coconut Shrimp

Servings: 4

Cooking Time: 12 Minutes

**Ingredients:**

- 1 pound large shrimp (about 16 to 20), peeled and de-veined
- ½ cup flour
- salt and freshly ground black pepper
- 2 egg whites
- ½ cup fine breadcrumbs
- ½ cup shredded unsweetened coconut
- zest of one lime
- ½ teaspoon salt
- ⅛ to ¼ teaspoon ground cayenne pepper
- vegetable or canola oil
- sweet chili sauce or duck sauce (for serving)

**Directions:**

1. Set up a dredging station. Place the flour in a shallow dish and season well with salt and freshly ground black pepper. Whisk the egg whites in a second shallow dish. In a third shallow dish, combine the breadcrumbs, coconut, lime zest, salt and cayenne pepper.

2. Preheat the air fryer to 400°F.

3. Dredge each shrimp first in the flour, then dip it in the egg mixture, and finally press it into the breadcrumb-coconut mixture to coat all sides. Place the breaded shrimp on a plate or baking sheet and spray both sides with vegetable oil.

4. Air-fry the shrimp in two batches, being sure not to over-crowd the basket. Air-fry for 5 minutes, turning the shrimp over for the last minute or two. Repeat with the second batch of shrimp.

5. Lower the temperature of the air fryer to 340°F. Return the first batch of shrimp to the air fryer basket with the second batch and air-fry for an additional 2 minutes, just to re-heat everything.

6. Serve with sweet chili sauce, duck sauce or just eat them plain!

# Curried Sweet-and-spicy Scallops

Servings:3

Cooking Time: 5 Minutes

**Ingredients:**

- ➤ 6 tablespoons Thai sweet chili sauce
- ➤ 2 cups (from about 5 cups cereal) Crushed Rice Krispies or other rice-puff cereal
- ➤ 2 teaspoons Yellow curry powder, purchased or homemade (see here)
- ➤ 1 pound Sea scallops
- ➤ Vegetable oil spray

**Directions:**

1. Preheat the air fryer to 400°F.

2. Set up and fill two shallow soup plates or small pie plates on your counter: one for the chili sauce and one for crumbs, mixed with the curry powder.

3. Dip a scallop into the chili sauce, coating it on all sides. Set it in the cereal mixture and turn several times to coat evenly. Gently shake off any excess and set the scallop on a cutting board. Continue dipping and coating the remaining scallops. Coat them all on all sides with the vegetable oil spray.

4. Set the scallops in the basket with as much air space between them as possible. Air-fry undisturbed for 5 minutes, or until lightly browned and crunchy.

5. Remove the basket. Set aside for 2 minutes to let the coating set up. Then gently pour the contents of the basket onto a platter and serve at once.

# Horseradish Crusted Salmon

Servings: 2

Cooking Time: 14 Minutes

**Ingredients:**

- 2 (5-ounce) salmon fillets
- salt and freshly ground black pepper
- 2 teaspoons Dijon mustard
- ½ cup panko breadcrumbs*
- 2 tablespoons prepared horseradish
- ½ teaspoon finely chopped lemon zest
- 1 tablespoon olive oil
- 1 tablespoon chopped fresh parsley

**Directions:**

1. Preheat the air fryer to 360°F.

2. Season the salmon with salt and freshly ground black pepper. Then spread the Dijon mustard on the salmon, coating the entire surface.

3. Combine the breadcrumbs, horseradish, lemon zest and olive oil in a small bowl. Spread the mixture over the top of the salmon and press down lightly with your hands, adhering it to the salmon using the mustard as "glue".

4. Transfer the salmon to the air fryer basket and air-fry at 360°F for 14 minutes (depending on how thick your fillet is) or until the fish feels firm to the touch. Sprinkle with the parsley.

# SANDWICHES AND BURGERS RECIPES

## Inside-out Cheeseburgers

Servings: 3

Cooking Time: 9-11 Minutes

**Ingredients:**

- 1 pound 2 ounces 90% lean ground beef
- ¾ teaspoon Dried oregano
- ¾ teaspoon Table salt
- ¾ teaspoon Ground black pepper
- ¼ teaspoon Garlic powder
- 6 tablespoons (about 1½ ounces) Shredded Cheddar, Swiss, or other semi-firm cheese, or a purchased blend of shredded cheeses
- 3 Hamburger buns (gluten-free, if a concern), split open

**Directions:**

1. Preheat the air fryer to 375°F .

2. Gently mix the ground beef, oregano, salt, pepper, and garlic powder in a bowl until well combined without turning the mixture to mush. Form it into two 6-inch patties for the small batch, three for the medium, or four for the large.

3. Place 2 tablespoons of the shredded cheese in the center of each patty. With clean hands, fold the sides of the patty up to cover the cheese, then pick it up and roll it gently into a ball to seal the cheese inside. Gently press it back into a 5-inch burger without letting any cheese squish out. Continue filling and preparing more burgers, as needed.

4. Place the burgers in the basket in one layer and air-fry undisturbed for 8 minutes for medium or 10 minutes for well-done. (An instant-read meat thermometer won't work for these burgers because it will hit the mostly melted cheese inside and offer a hotter temperature than the surrounding meat.)

5. Use a nonstick-safe spatula, and perhaps a flatware fork for balance, to transfer the burgers to a cutting board. Set the buns cut side down in the basket in one layer (working in batches as necessary) and air-fry undisturbed for 1 minute, to toast a bit and warm up. Cool the burgers a few minutes more, then serve them warm in the buns.

# Thai-style Pork Sliders

Servings: 4

Cooking Time: 15 Minutes

**Ingredients:**

- ➢ 11 ounces Ground pork
- ➢ 2½ tablespoons Very thinly sliced scallions, white and green parts
- ➢ 4 teaspoons Minced peeled fresh ginger
- ➢ 2½ teaspoons Fish sauce (gluten-free, if a concern)
- ➢ 2 teaspoons Thai curry paste (see the headnote; gluten-free, if a concern)
- ➢ 2 teaspoons Light brown sugar
- ➢ ¾ teaspoon Ground black pepper
- ➢ 4 Slider buns (gluten-free, if a concern)

**Directions:**

1. Preheat the air fryer to 375°F .

2. Gently mix the pork, scallions, ginger, fish sauce, curry paste, brown sugar, and black pepper in a bowl until well combined. With clean, wet hands, form about ⅓ cup of the pork mixture into a slider about 2½ inches in diameter. Repeat until you use up all the meat—3 sliders for the small batch, 4 for the medium, and 6 for the large. (Keep wetting your hands to help the patties adhere.)

3. When the machine is at temperature, set the sliders in the basket in one layer. Air-fry undisturbed for 14 minutes, or until the sliders are golden brown and caramelized at their edges and an instant-read meat thermometer inserted into the center of a slider registers 160°F.

4. Use a nonstick-safe spatula, and perhaps a flatware fork for balance, to transfer the sliders to a cutting board. Set the buns cut side down in the basket in one layer (working in batches as necessary) and air-fry undisturbed for 1 minute, to toast a bit and warm up. Serve the sliders warm in the buns.

# Perfect Burgers

Servings: 3

Cooking Time: 13 Minutes

**Ingredients:**

- ➢ 1 pound 2 ounces 90% lean ground beef
- ➢ 1½ tablespoons Worcestershire sauce (gluten-free, if a concern)
- ➢ ½ teaspoon Ground black pepper
- ➢ 3 Hamburger buns (gluten-free if a concern), split open

**Directions:**

1. Preheat the air fryer to 375°F .

2. Gently mix the ground beef, Worcestershire sauce, and pepper in a bowl until well combined but preserving as much of the meat's fibers as possible. Divide this mixture into two 5-inch patties for the small batch, three 5-inch patties for the medium, or four 5-inch patties for the large. Make a thumbprint indentation in the center of each patty, about halfway through the meat.

3. Set the patties in the basket in one layer with some space between them. Air-fry undisturbed for 10 minutes, or until an instant-read meat thermometer inserted into the center of a burger registers 160°F (a medium-well burger). You may need to add 2 minutes cooking time if the air fryer is at 360°F.

4. Use a nonstick-safe spatula, and perhaps a flatware fork for balance, to transfer the burgers to a cutting board. Set the buns cut side down in the basket in one layer (working in batches as necessary) and air-fry undisturbed for 1 minute, to toast a bit and warm up. Serve the burgers in the warm buns.

# Best-ever Roast Beef Sandwiches

Servings: 6

Cooking Time: 30-50 Minutes

**Ingredients:**

- 2½ teaspoons Olive oil
- 1½ teaspoons Dried oregano
- 1½ teaspoons Dried thyme
- 1½ teaspoons Onion powder
- 1½ teaspoons Table salt
- 1½ teaspoons Ground black pepper
- 3 pounds Beef eye of round
- 6 Round soft rolls, such as Kaiser rolls or hamburger buns (gluten-free, if a concern), split open lengthwise
- ¾ cup Regular, low-fat, or fat-free mayonnaise (gluten-free, if a concern)
- 6 Romaine lettuce leaves, rinsed
- 6 Round tomato slices (¼ inch thick)

**Directions:**

1. Preheat the air fryer to 350°F .

2. Mix the oil, oregano, thyme, onion powder, salt, and pepper in a small bowl. Spread this mixture all over the eye of round.

3. When the machine is at temperature, set the beef in the basket and air-fry for 30 to 50 minutes (the range depends on the size of the cut), turning the meat twice, until an instant-read meat thermometer inserted into the thickest piece of the meat registers 130°F for rare, 140°F for medium, or 150°F for well-done.

4. Use kitchen tongs to transfer the beef to a cutting board. Cool for 10 minutes. If serving now, carve into ⅛-inch-thick slices. Spread each roll with 2 tablespoons mayonnaise and divide the beef slices between the rolls. Top with a lettuce leaf and a tomato slice and serve. Or set the beef in a container, cover, and refrigerate for up to 3 days to make cold roast beef sandwiches anytime.

# Dijon Thyme Burgers



Cooking Time: 18 Minutes

**Ingredients:**

- 1 pound lean ground beef
- ⅓ cup panko breadcrumbs
- ¼ cup finely chopped onion
- 3 tablespoons Dijon mustard
- 1 tablespoon chopped fresh thyme
- 4 teaspoons Worcestershire sauce
- 1 teaspoon salt
- freshly ground black pepper
- Topping (optional):
- 2 tablespoons Dijon mustard
- 1 tablespoon dark brown sugar
- 1 teaspoon Worcestershire sauce
- 4 ounces sliced Swiss cheese, optional

**Directions:**

1. Combine all the burger ingredients together in a large bowl and mix well. Divide the meat into 4 equal portions and then form the burgers, being careful not to over-handle the meat. One good way to do this is to throw the meat back and forth from one hand to another, packing the meat each time you catch it. Flatten the balls into patties, making an indentation in the center of each patty with your thumb (this will help it stay flat as it cooks) and flattening the sides of the burgers so that they will fit nicely into the air fryer basket.

2. Preheat the air fryer to 370°F.

3. If you don't have room for all four burgers, air-fry two or three burgers at a time for 8 minutes. Flip the burgers over and air-fry for another 6 minutes.

4. While the burgers are cooking combine the Dijon mustard, dark brown sugar, and Worcestershire sauce in a small bowl and mix well. This optional topping to the burgers really adds a boost of flavor at the end. Spread the Dijon topping evenly on each burger. If you cooked the burgers in batches, return the first batch to the cooker at this time – it's ok to place the fourth burger on top of the others in the center of the basket. Air-fry the burgers for another 3 minutes.

5. Finally, if desired, top each burger with a slice of Swiss cheese. Lower the air fryer temperature to 330°F and air-fry for another minute to melt the cheese. Serve the burgers on toasted brioche buns, dressed the way you like them.

# Lamb Burgers

Servings: 3

Cooking Time: 17 Minutes

**Ingredients:**

- ➢ 1 pound 2 ounces Ground lamb
- ➢ 3 tablespoons Crumbled feta
- ➢ 1 teaspoon Minced garlic
- ➢ 1 teaspoon Tomato paste
- ➢ ¾ teaspoon Ground coriander
- ➢ ¾ teaspoon Ground dried ginger
- ➢ Up to ⅛ teaspoon Cayenne
- ➢ Up to a ⅛ teaspoon Table salt (optional)
- ➢ 3 Kaiser rolls or hamburger buns (gluten-free, if a concern), split open

**Directions:**

1. Preheat the air fryer to 375°F .

2. Gently mix the ground lamb, feta, garlic, tomato paste, coriander, ginger, cayenne, and salt (if using) in a bowl until well combined, trying to keep the bits of cheese intact. Form this mixture into two 5-inch patties for the small batch, three 5-inch patties for the medium, or four 5-inch patties for the large.

3. Set the patties in the basket in one layer and air-fry undisturbed for 16 minutes, or until an instant-read meat thermometer inserted into one burger registers 160°F. (The cheese is not an issue with the temperature probe in this recipe as it was for the Inside-Out Cheeseburgers, because the feta is so well mixed into the ground meat.)

4. Use a nonstick-safe spatula, and perhaps a flatware fork for balance, to transfer the burgers to a cutting board. Set the buns cut side down in the basket in one layer (working in batches as necessary) and air-fry undisturbed for 1 minute, to toast a bit and warm up. Serve the burgers warm in the buns.

# Salmon Burgers

Servings: 3

Cooking Time: 8 Minutes

**Ingredients:**

- ➢ 1 pound 2 ounces Skinless salmon fillet, preferably fattier Atlantic salmon
- ➢ 1½ tablespoons Minced chives or the green part of a scallion
- ➢ ½ cup Plain panko bread crumbs (gluten-free, if a concern)
- ➢ 1½ teaspoons Dijon mustard (gluten-free, if a concern)
- ➢ 1½ teaspoons Drained and rinsed capers, minced
- ➢ 1½ teaspoons Lemon juice
- ➢ ¼ teaspoon Table salt
- ➢ ¼ teaspoon Ground black pepper
- ➢ Vegetable oil spray

**Directions:**

1. Preheat the air fryer to 375°F .

2. Cut the salmon into pieces that will fit in a food processor. Cover and pulse until coarsely chopped. Add the chives and pulse to combine, until the fish is ground but not a paste. Scrape down and remove the blade. Scrape the salmon mixture into a bowl. Add the bread crumbs, mustard, capers, lemon juice, salt, and pepper. Stir gently until well combined.

3. Use clean and dry hands to form the mixture into two 5-inch patties for a small batch, three 5-inch patties for a medium batch, or four 5-inch patties for a large one.

4. Coat both sides of each patty with vegetable oil spray. Set them in the basket in one layer and air-fry undisturbed for 8 minutes, or until browned and an instant-read meat thermometer inserted into the center of a burger registers 145°F.

5. Use a nonstick-safe spatula, and perhaps a flatware fork for balance, to transfer the burgers to a wire rack. Cool for 2 or 3 minutes before serving.

# Chicken Gyros

Servings: 4

Cooking Time: 14 Minutes

**Ingredients:**

- ➤ 4 4- to 5-ounce boneless skinless chicken thighs, trimmed of any fat blobs
- ➤ 2 tablespoons Lemon juice
- ➤ 2 tablespoons Red wine vinegar
- ➤ 2 tablespoons Olive oil
- ➤ 2 teaspoons Dried oregano
- ➤ 2 teaspoons Minced garlic
- ➤ 1 teaspoon Table salt
- ➤ 1 teaspoon Ground black pepper
- ➤ 4 Pita pockets (gluten-free, if a concern)
- ➤ ½ cup Chopped tomatoes
- ➤ ½ cup Bottled regular, low-fat, or fat-free ranch dressing (gluten-free, if a concern)

**Directions:**

1.  Mix the thighs, lemon juice, vinegar, oil, oregano, garlic, salt, and pepper in a zip-closed bag. Seal, gently massage the marinade into the meat through the plastic, and refrigerate for at least 2 hours or up to 6 hours. (Longer than that and the meat can turn rubbery.)

2.  Set the plastic bag out on the counter (to make the contents a little less frigid). Preheat the air fryer to 375°F.

3.  When the machine is at temperature, use kitchen tongs to place the thighs in the basket in one layer. Discard the marinade. Air-fry the chicken thighs undisturbed for 12 minutes, or until browned and an instant-read meat thermometer inserted into the thickest part of one thigh registers 165°F. You may need to air-fry the chicken 2 minutes longer if the machine's temperature is 360°F.

4.  Use kitchen tongs to transfer the thighs to a cutting board. Cool for 5 minutes, then set one thigh in each of the pita pockets. Top each with 2 tablespoons chopped tomatoes and 2 tablespoons dressing. Serve warm.

Printed by Libri Plureos GmbH in Hamburg,
Germany